The

SPIRIT
SHOP

conquering addiction through the power of the
Holy Spirit

ANDREW POTTER

DEDICATION AND ACKNOWLEDGEMENTS:

This work is dedicated to all of my friends who have shared my pathway and added to my joy, especially my wife and best friend; Diane Potter.

Proverbs 31:29 (NIV): Many women do noble things, but you surpass them all.

Cover Art: Diane Potter

And to Patrick and Christopher, my kindred spirits:

1 John 3:16 (NIV): This is how we know what love is: Jesus Christ laid down his life for us. And we ought to lay down our lives for our brothers.

Edited by Marie Ackerman:

Matthew 6:28-29 (NIV): See how the lilies of the field grow. They do not labor or spin. Yet I tell you that not even Solomon in all his splendor was dressed like one of these.

INDEX:

FORWARD:

*I*s mere willpower enough to overcome your addictive and destructive lifestyle? In his new, heart-inspiring and challenging book, Andrew Potter points the way to genuine freedom and liberating joy through experiencing the power of God's Holy Spirit found only in a vital relationship with Jesus Christ.

Here, you will not find all the typical trite platitudes and self-help formulas of an arm-chair theorist normally associated with those in our day, seeking to address hard life issues such as addiction. Instead, you'll find the depth of insight that can only come from someone who knows first-hand both the bondage of addiction and the liberating freedom of redemption in Christ. Here, you'll find true hope for lasting change.

Let me encourage you to take Andrew Potter up on his provocative challenge to begin your journey to freedom by first just stepping inside *The Spirit Shop*. Then, once you're inside, dare to set aside all your previous perceptions regarding how to change—and begin perusing, thoughtfully and prayerfully, each one of *The Spirit Shop's* aisles.

As you do, leave behind, on the shelves at the end of each aisle, all those items that have hindered you for so long. And then add to your cart, by God's grace, all those items through which you can conquer your addictions and destructive lifestyles by the power of the Holy Spirit.

You will never be the same.

Dr. Steven L. Childers
Associate Professor of Practical Theology
Reformed Theological Seminary –Orlando, Florida

PREFACE

*H*ow many times have you attempted to quit a negative behavior, an addiction or a destructive lifestyle; only to fall victim to it again by the failed efforts of utilizing your own willpower? Are you tired of trying and failing through your own accord? If you are truly ready to quit, this is your salvation; the solution rests within the power of the Holy Spirit, and not by your own inadequate efforts.

The Apostle Paul speaks of a freedom from this frustration in *Romans 7: 5-6 (NIV): "For when we were controlled by the sinful nature, the sinful passions aroused by the law were at work in our bodies, so that we bore fruit for death. But now, by dying to what once bound us, we have been released from the law so that we serve in the new way of the Spirit, and not in the old way of the written code."*

I would like to invite you to step inside *The Spirit Shop* and experience genuine freedom as well as the ability to finally possess a liberating joy through the power of the Holy Spirit, enabling you to rediscover your true self; the individual God designed you to be through his Son Jesus Christ.

The invitation would not be complete without a bit of a warning; which is the fact that within the walls of *The Spirit Shop* you will find real life experiences. This is not your disguised Sunday school lesson tailored to the "adult Christian reader," designed to get everybody back in church. And therefore, some of it may be a little hard to swallow for the typical "religious" crowd. But this is an opportunity to heal your spirit and therefore receive the abundance and peace that accompanies the life God intended you to live.

Already confused? Jesus Christ explains it to the Pharisees, the "religious leaders" of his time, a little differently, but I believe you will see the same point: *Mark 2: 16-17 (NIV): When the teachers of the law who were Pharisees saw him eating with the "sinners" and tax collectors, they asked his disciples: "Why does he eat with tax collectors and 'sinners'?" On hearing this, Jesus said to them, "It is not the healthy who need a doctor, but the sick. I have not come to call the righteous, but sinners."* Of course the irony of the answer Christ offers, lies in the fact that none of us are righteous; we are all sinners, including the church going religious types of the past, present and future.

No matter how you interpret or define the degree of your present condition, the reality is that within the natural spirit of man, we are not only all sick, but terminally ill. So before you get out of the car and make your way through the parking lot, I need to ask you about one other thing, but I will call on Christ to pose the question: *John 5:6 (NIV): When Jesus saw him lying there and learned that he had been in this condition for a long time, he asked him, "Do you want to get well?"*

Now, if you are like me, as you dart into the store with your dark sunglasses on, don't forget to get a shopping cart (open mind) when entering. The shopping cart will allow you to really take your time as you peruse the 13 Aisles of *The Spirit Shop*. Be sure to read the banner at the front of each aisle, which will give you a general idea of what you may find on that particular aisle. At the end of each aisle you will see suggestions as to items you may want to "Leave on Shelf" or "Add to Cart," and finally a "Prayer Point" for further contemplation and direction.

So welcome to the store and enjoy your shopping experience as you enter:

The Spirit Shop: Where hope gives wings to the imagination and faith lends the power to fly.

AISLE ONE

Discovery

I am broken. My spirit is weak and I have lost my way.

Jeremiah 8:11 (NIV): They dress the wound of my people as though it were not serious. "Peace, peace," they say, when there is no peace.

⚜

*M*y favorite literary works written by mortal men are: Peter Pan; for the concept of remaining an eternal child at heart, and the Wizard of Oz; for the assurance that we have always had the ability within our hearts to reach our true home.

I am pleased to report that God's book, the Holy Bible, provides us with the true reality of the former two, through his merciful love, the sacrifice of his Son, and the graceful offering of the Holy Spirit.

Christ tells us in *Matthew 18* that unless you become like a child, you will never enter the kingdom of heaven and then underlines the fact by explaining that whoever humbles himself like a child is the greatest in the kingdom of heaven.

Therefore, the Apostle Paul's description of his own Christian transition in *1 Corinthians 13:11(NIV): "When I was a child, I talked like a child; I thought like a child, I reasoned like a child. When I became a man, I put childish ways behind me,"* would appear to be in direct conflict with the path of salvation Christ outlines in *Matthew 18*. This perceived conflict is soon dismissed once you consider the fact that many of the childish things Paul is pleading with us to relinquish are the very things that prevent us from becoming like a child at heart and subsequently obscuring the doorway to our true home.

Jesus Christ describes becoming like a child another way in *John 3: 5-6 (NIV)*, as he responds to Nicodemus, who is confused in regard to the fact that "becoming like a child" actually involves being born again: *Jesus answered, "I tell you the truth, no one can enter the kingdom of God unless he is born of water and the Spirit. Flesh gives birth to flesh, but the Spirit gives birth to spirit."*

It becomes clear that Paul is on the same path as Christ when we continue to read *1 Corinthians 13: 12-13 (NIV): "Now we see but a poor reflection as in a mirror; then we shall see face to face. Now, I know in part; then I shall know fully, even as I am fully known."* God knows your spirit, because the Spirit is his: the Holy Spirit. We have inherited the Holy Spirit through the righteousness Christ gave each and every one of us by his sacrifice on the cross for our sins.

LEAVE ON SHELF:

Leave the negative issues and harmful behavior in the past, as these are not only destructive, but prohibitive in regard to reaching your true potential in Christ.

ADD TO CART:

Discover your true spirit, which is the Holy Spirit within you, and consequently the person God created you to be.

The old saying, "You can never go home again," is not really accurate, once we discover our true home within the Holy Spirit. Christ not only calls us to become like children in order to enter the kingdom of heaven, but in keeping with the childhood theme, offers us the ultimate "Do-Over" in order to achieve this. Once we step out in faith, accepting Christ as our Savior, he ordains us with our true spirit; the Holy Spirit within us. It is at that very moment, through the heart of a child, that we catch our first starry eyed glimpse of the genuine and complete person God created us to be.

John 8:32 (NIV): Then you will know the truth, and the truth will set you free.

PRAYER POINT:

Direct me in the honest assessment of my past as I live within the present hope and love of Christ. Teach me to eliminate negative conformity, while recognizing new opportunities. Instruct me to embrace change within the power of the Holy Spirit.

AISLE TWO

Definition

Purpose and meaning have vanished within a sea of constant and mundane necessity.

Psalm 121: 1-2 (NIV): I lift up my eyes to the hills —where does my help come from? My help comes from the Lord, the Maker of heaven and earth.

*T*he Holy Spirit is with God the Father and Jesus Christ the Son from the beginning: *Genesis 1: 1-4 (KJV):*

In the beginning God created the heaven and the earth. And the earth was without form and void; and darkness was upon the face of the deep. And the Spirit of God (Holy Spirit) *moved upon the face of the waters. And God said* (God spoke the Word), *"Let there be light," and there was light. And God saw the light, that it was good: and God divided the light from the darkness.* (Christ is the Word, God spoke the Word: *John 1:1 (NIV): "In the beginning was the Word, and the Word was with God, and the Word was God.")*

God sent his Son Jesus Christ, into the world to die for our sins through the power of the Holy Spirit: *Luke 1: 34-35 (NIV):*

"How will this be," Mary asked the angel, "since I am a virgin?" The angel answered, "The Holy Spirit will come upon you, and the power of the Most High will overshadow you. So the holy one to be born will be called the Son of God."

The Holy Spirit descended upon Jesus the moment after his baptism: *Matthew 3: 16-17 (NIV):*

As soon as Jesus was baptized, he went up out of the water. At that moment heaven was opened, and he saw the Spirit of God descending like a dove and lighting on him. And a voice from heaven said, "This is my Son, whom I love; with him I am well pleased."

After Christ died on the cross for our sins, and rose from the dead, he appeared to his disciples, giving them the promise of the Holy Spirit's power: *Luke 24: 45-49 (NIV):*

Then he opened their minds, so they could understand the Scriptures. He told them, "This is what is written: The Christ will suffer and rise from the dead on the third day, and repentance and forgiveness of sins will be preached in his name to all nations, beginning at Jerusalem. You are witnesses of these things. I am going to send you what my Father has promised (The Holy Spirit)*; but stay in the city until you have been clothed with power* (The Holy Spirit) *from on high."* (The power from on high is the Holy Spirit: *Acts 1: 4-5 (NIV): On one occasion, while he was eating with them, he gave them this command: "Do not leave Jerusalem but wait for the gift my Father promised, which you have heard me speak about. For John baptized with water, but in a few days you will be baptized with the Holy Spirit.")*

The Apostle Paul glorifies the omniscience (infinite knowledge) and the omnipotence (infinite power) of the Holy Spirit through his preaching. The fact that Paul gives us thirteen of the twenty seven books of the New Testament, magnifies the omnipresence (infinite presence) that is ours today, through the Spirit: *1 Corinthians 2: 4-5 (NIV):*

> *"My message and my preaching were not with wise and persuasive words, but with a demonstration of the Spirit's power, so that your faith might not rest on men's wisdom, but on God's power."*

From the time we were first exposed to "religion" or heard "The Gospel," which are often two entirely different concepts, we have found ourselves to be severely inadequate when it comes to obedience. Unfortunately, this has often resulted in disengaging ourselves from the Gospel of Christ and the subsequent power of the Holy Spirit, due to the fact that we cannot adhere to the "religion of the law" by our own accord. The "Good News" is that we only need to accept by faith the salvation Christ offers us by his sacrifice for our "inadequacies," and the power to obey is ours through his love within the Holy Spirit: *John 14: 24-27(NIV):*

> *"He who does not love me will not obey my teaching. These words you hear are not my own; they belong to the Father who sent me. All this I have spoken while still with you. But the Counselor, the Holy Spirit, whom the Father will send in my name, will teach you all things and will remind you of everything I have said to you. Peace I leave with you; my peace I give you. I do not give to you as the world gives. Do not let your hearts be troubled and do not be afraid."*

The Holy Spirit is the power to not only love, but to obey; passed down from the Father, and made possible by the sacrifice of the Son: *John 15:9-12 (NIV):*

> *"As the Father has loved me, so have I loved you. Now remain in my love. If you obey my commands, you will remain in my love, just as I have obeyed my Father's commands and remain in his love. I have told you this so that my joy may be in you and that your joy may be complete. My command is this: Love each other as I have loved you.*

The Holy Spirit is the Alpha and the Omega, the beginning and the end. Just as he is present in the first chapter of the Bible, creating the heaven and the earth with God the Father and Christ the Son, he is present in the last chapter of the Bible; issuing an invitation for all to inherit eternal life by grace and faith in our Lord Jesus Christ: *Revelation 22: 16-17 (NIV):*

> *"I, Jesus, have sent my angel to give you this testimony for the churches. I am the Root and the Offspring of David, and the bright Morning Star." The Spirit and the bride say, "Come!" And let him who hears say, "Come!" Whoever is thirsty, let him come, and whoever wishes, let him take the free gift of the water of life.*

LEAVE ON SHELF:

Dismiss the false belief that you may not be worthy enough to accept and acknowledge the Holy Spirit within your life, after Christ died for your forgiveness; enabling you to accept this gift out of his grace, mercy and love.

ADD TO CART:

Realize the Holy Spirit's presence within God's Word; the Holy Bible, and his invitation to the "free gift" of salvation through his Son Jesus Christ.

Life is a series of escalating stipulations: "If you aren't nice, Santa Claus won't come." "If you don't finish school, you won't get a good job." "If you don't work, you won't get paid." "If you don't save your money, you can't retire." Then, if these weren't enough, you throw in the physical health qualifiers, which sometimes seem contradictory: "If you drink this, it builds strong bones." "If you drink this, it increases your cholesterol." "If you don't have strong bones you won't live very long." "If you have high cholesterol, you won't live very long." "If you don't eat this, you will die sooner than later." "If you drink this, it will kill you!"

This entire process we call life seems a little fatalistic at best. After all, even if we do everything "right" along the way, the final curtain, at least for this physical shell of a body, eventually falls on us all. Bearing this in mind, some choose to "eat, drink, and be merry," while others select a staunch religious route; where things are not so fun now, granted, but a type of insurance policy for the hereafter never seems to hurt. The staunch religious group is usually seen grimacing and secretly admiring the "eat, drink, and be merry" folks along the way. While the "eat, drink, and be merry" bunch continue to party, thoughts of mortality do begin to surface; so they usually pencil in a future date of conversion. But for the time being, the "eat, drink and be merry" crowd just want to have fun. A conscientious observer may wish for both worlds. After all, can you really blame someone for wanting to "have their cake and eat it too?" Well, perhaps you can have the best of both worlds. But since we are all living and breathing right now, let's first examine our mortality, which we all harbor in the back of our minds, whether we like to admit it or not.

Last but certainly not least, is the eternal caveat: *Genesis 2:16-17 (NIV): And the Lord God commanded the man, "You are free to eat from any tree in the garden; but you must not eat from the tree of the knowledge of good and evil, for when you eat of it you will surely die."* Oh Man! No pun intended, but where is that "Do-Over" from Aisle One when we really need it? After all, this opens up an entirely new can of worms in regard to escalating stipulations; or perhaps a can of worms the size of serpents in this instance. If we remember what happened in the Garden of Eden *(Genesis 2)*, Adam and Eve didn't do a very good job of being obedient children. And as a result of desiring to be 'all grown up' like God the Father, we have come full circle to the list of those escalating stipulations; beginning with being nice. Only in this case there is a lot more at stake than missing Santa Claus this Christmas: "You cannot go to heaven, if you're not a Christian." "You cannot really be a Christian, if you don't act like one." "If you become a Christian, you have to quit this and that," which generally first appears to involve anything fun. Does there have to be a catch to everything?

After wandering through this little wilderness of stipulations is it any wonder that man is the only creature that is fully aware of heaven, yet continues to live like hell? And while this line of questioning has probably kept more people out of church over the past two thousand years than boring sermons or religious hypocrites, we are left with some really 'good news' or great news in this case, which is the Gospel. Jesus Christ died on the Cross of Calvary for the redemption of all mankind. We are now forgiven for our sins and therefore made righteous in the eyes of God the Father, by accepting this salvation out of faith. So why do our lifestyles fail to portray this commitment? The answer lies within the power of the Holy Spirit. Christ has given you the Holy Spirit as a deposit. This deposit is an additional blessing as a result of your acceptance and belief in him as your personal Savior.

PRAYER POINT:

Lead me in the knowledge, power, love and awareness of the Holy Spirit. Make me aware of the fact that I leave my sins, as well as my apprehensions and misgivings at the foot of the cross. Grant me the wisdom of knowing, this will be the best of both worlds, with abundant joy on earth and an eternal legacy in heaven.

AISLE THREE

The Task

Conventional religion has failed me. I am no longer able to paint by the numbers; my palette is dry.

Isaiah 43:19 (NIV): See, I am doing a new thing! Now it springs up; do you not perceive it? I am making a way in the desert and streams in the wasteland.

❧

"*Then you will know that I am in Israel; that I am the Lord your God, and there is no other; never again will my people be shamed. And afterward, I will pour out my Spirit on all people.*" *Joel 2: 27-28 (NIV)*

God is making a promise of salvation to a people who have been unfaithful. The Israelite's main offense was apparently idol worship, but we may rest assured there were probably a few other blemishes on their resume. The Apostle Paul puts the possibilities down in black and white as he lists them in *Galatians 5:19: "The acts of the sinful nature are obvious: sexual immorality, impurity and debauchery, idolatry and witchcraft; hatred, discord, jealousy, fits of rage, selfish ambition, dissensions, factions and envy; drunkenness, orgies and the like."*

If you honestly think about the laundry list Paul lays down in Galatians chapter five you can probably plug yourself in to a few more than you would have hoped to claim, or at least admit to on any given Sunday, as you glad hand your way to your usual spot on the old church pew. The sad part about that for most of us is that I am just talking about our performance over the past week.

By now you are probably re-reading the list to determine just what you are getting yourself in to as you continue to consider Paul's list of "No – No's". Let me assure you that we are all in this together. As the old saying goes, "I never claimed to be a saint, but simply a forgiven sinner." If we could just stop there, then there would be very little reason for change. But the problem lies in the repeat offenses, even after we have accepted the gift of salvation from our Lord Jesus Christ.

Paul even speaks to this problem of serial sin in *Romans 7: 14-20 (NIV): "As it is, it is no longer I myself who do it, but sin living in me. I know that nothing good lives in me, that is, in my sinful nature. For I have the desire to do what is good; but I cannot carry it out. For what I do is not the good I want to do; no, the evil I do not want to do-this I keep on doing. Now if I do what I do not want to do, it is no longer I who do it, but it is sin living in me that does it."*

So how does one go about making their way over to the list found in *Galatians 5:22; love, joy, peace, patience, kindness, goodness, faithfulness, gentleness and self-control* ? Paul actually gives you a big hint, in Galatians 5:22, right before he lays down the "do good" list, when he defines the list as "fruit of the Spirit." After all, you have to admit the grass definitely does look "evergreen" on the other side. Or perhaps that is "forever green," just to hedge one's eternal bet.

But how do we get there, and more importantly, how do we stay? Therein lies the problem which most of us do a very good job of ignoring as we launch voyage after "titanic" voyage under our own strength and endurance in a futile attempt to reach these other shores. And, if you will allow me one last sailing metaphor, wind up hopelessly crashing "on the rocks." This brings me back to the "No-No" list in *Galatians 5:19*, but specifically focusing on "drunkenness." The Bible appears to have more to say about this act of the sinful nature than the other fourteen Paul lists in Galatians 5, so our primary focus will be spirit overindulgence.

If you do not have a battle with excessive grapes, feel free to interject your own frequently visited vice; and for a "growing" number of Americans, it could be right in front of you:

For drunkards and gluttons become poor and drowsiness clothes them in rags. Proverbs 23:21(NIV)

Do not join those who drink too much wine or gorge themselves on meat. Proverbs 23:20 (NIV)

If you are still in denial as to the interchanging of your sin: one for the other, then here is one last scripture to "weigh-in" with:

"For, as I have often told you before and now say again even with tears, many live as enemies of the cross of Christ. Their destiny is destruction, their god is their stomach, and their glory is in their shame. Their mind is on earthly things. But our citizenship is in heaven. And we eagerly await a Savior from there, the Lord Jesus Christ, who, by the power that enables him to bring everything under his control, will transform our lowly bodies so that they will be like his glorious body." Philippians 3: 18-21 (NIV)

In case you missed it, the *"power that enables him"* is the same power God gave us through him: The Holy Spirit.

LEAVE ON SHELF:

Most of us try to grind it out on our own accord, believing we can eliminate the acts of the sinful nature, due to the fact that we are, after all, Christians by definition. These efforts, utilizing our own willpower exclusively, are destined to end in failure.

ADD TO CART:

The fruit of the Holy Spirit may only be obtained and maintained by the power of the Holy Spirit within you.

This decision should actually be pretty simple. We opt for the power of the Holy Spirit internally, rather than winding up with this monumental struggle of going it on our own. So I guess the fact that I have had to make this decision over and over again is what really amazes me. At the end of the day, it speaks well for the persuasive power of our own human spirits, which is exactly how this sinful nature "snaked" its way into this world in the first place. Eve, soon followed by Adam, were the first ones to make this decision that they may be better off without all this spiritual baggage. I can just imagine what they must have been thinking because it is the same thought process I go through before one of these misguided voyages. It usually begins with something like this: "OK, I am familiar enough with the lay of the land here, and after all, I am just as smart as the next guy, so I can drink once more; in moderation that is."

Even though it was not "excessive spirits" or the "all you can eat buffet" that caused Adam and Eve to receive the eviction notice, it was that initial bite out of the "bad apple" of substituting their perceived wisdom and power for God's. When you consider sin, either before or after the fact, you will always discover the common denominator is the drive to satisfy a perceived need. This desire has to be fulfilled apart from God, in order to satisfy our natural and often savage ego. In the back of our minds, we are fully aware that God wants nothing to do with it, but soon drown this assumption in a sea of natural lust.

So whenever we make this ill-fated decision to go it on our own, the four of us always wind up with the same results. Adam and Eve, as well as you and me, are trading the Holy Spirit for the spirit of the natural man. We are cashing in faith, obedience and love, for despair, envy, anxiety and discouragement, which is a bad bargain in anyone's book. We make the decision to be a "somebody," leaving the Body of Christ in our wake. And to add insult to injury, we assume the worst, which is the ill-conceived notion that God may very well be out for revenge. Instead of opting to become like a child in God's Kingdom, we leave the power of the Holy Spirit behind; and soon find ourselves in the ultimate childhood game of "hide and seek": *Genesis 3: 8-10 (NIV): Then the man and his wife heard the sound of the Lord God as he was walking in the garden in the cool of the day, and they hid from the Lord God among the trees of the garden. But the Lord God called to the man, "Where are you?" He answered, "I heard you in the garden, and I was afraid because I was naked; so I hid."*

Yes, we soon discover when we set out to conquer this earthly kingdom through our own wisdom and power that we are not only ill-equipped to face the challenge, but we find ourselves simply naked when it comes to fighting without the armor of the Holy Spirit.

PRAYER POINT:

Teach me to celebrate my alliance with the Holy Spirit; constantly calling upon his power and wisdom. Help me to recognize battlefields before conflicts arise, so that I may rest in your sanctuary, and find my strength within your almighty presence.

AISLE FOUR

Two Questions

At first glance the road before me is overwhelming. The mirage of past failures makes it difficult to chart a course; to take that initial step of faith into the abyss.

Jeremiah 12:5 (NIV): If you have raced with men on foot and they have worn you out, how can you compete with horses? If you stumble in safe country, how will you manage in thickets by the Jordan?

Jeremiah 10:23 (NIV): I know, O Lord, that a man's life is not his own; it is not for man to direct his steps.

The question that Paul asks the folks that continue to sin with a vengeance in *Galatians 3: 2-3*, ranks second on the list of the "all time" most important questions we may ask ourselves. The most important question would be: "How do I achieve eternal salvation?" Answer: *John 3:16 (NIV): "For God so loved the world that he gave his one and only Son, that whoever believes in him shall not perish but have eternal life."*

If you are having a hard time believing in this one, then I would respectfully request that you pray over *Job 33:4(NIV): "The Spirit of God has made me; the breath of the Almighty gives me life."*

Pray this Scripture to the Almighty God, asking him to send you insight and wisdom, and to open your heart toward his Word. *Jeremiah 33:2-3 (NIV): "This is what the Lord says, he who made the earth, the Lord who formed it and established it – the Lord is his name: 'Call to me and I will answer you and tell you great and unsearchable things you do not know.'"*

Trust in God and you will never be disappointed by sincerely praying this prayer. Ask God to show you his path for your eternal salvation and abundant life through his Son Jesus Christ and the Bible; the living Word of God. Ask God to show you the necessity to accept his Son, who died on the cross for the sins of mankind, so that God will view us as spotless when it comes to our sin. Once you have sincerely prayed to accept Christ Jesus into your life as your personal Savior; having accepted God's gift of grace out of your faith, you receive the Holy Spirit. The Holy Spirit is the very Person of God the Father and his Son Jesus Christ, dwelling inside you.

But the problem that most Christians experience within their daily lives is the fact that they are trying to follow the law: The Ten Commandments, as well as Paul's list of "do's and don'ts" that we see in *Galatians*, by their own power. This exercise of our own willpower is futile at best. By doing this, you are turning your back on God's greatest gift since his Son, which is the power of the Holy Spirit.

So please acknowledge my evangelistic detour here and let's move on to the "runner up" on the "all time" most important Biblical questions list:

"I would like to learn just one thing from you: Did you receive the Spirit by observing the law or by believing what you heard? Are you so foolish, after beginning with the Spirit, are you now trying to obtain your goal by human effort." Galatians 3: 2-3 (NIV)

In other words, you have accepted the Lord Jesus Christ, God's Son, as your Lord and Savior out of faith. Through that sincere acceptance you have invited him to live within you. Now you are righteous through the sacrifice of Jesus Christ on the Cross of Calvary for your sins. As a result of that faith, God has given you the Holy Spirit. The Holy Spirit is a tremendous weapon for us to utilize in the battle to be obedient. Then, most of us turn right around and ignore or never ask the Holy Spirit for help again. We try with all of "our" might to follow this law like any natural man. Why "on earth" would we even attempt this, when we possess the "One" true power that will prevail every time? The Holy Bible even gives us the final results of this matchup: *1 John 4:4 (NIV): Greater is he that is in you, than he who is in the world.*

If you are looking for a secular approach to this ill-conceived plan based on your own efforts, this is like discovering you have an NFL quarterback on your football team and then making the conscious decision to be the signal caller yourself or perhaps you have a gourmet chef in the kitchen relegated to peeling onions. Not to leave the NASCAR fans out; discovering you have a circuit driver in the pits while you take the multi-million dollar modified stockcar into the wall. I think you get the point by now. But the final assessment involves multiplying these misguided efforts by infinity, in order to perceive the negative impact of substituting your willpower for that of the Holy Spirit's power. Speaking of sports and scores, another old coach once said: *"Not by might nor by power, but by my Spirit, says the Lord Almighty." Zechariah 3: 6 (NIV).*

Now that we have the car packed; eternal salvation through Christ, and know the general proximity of the gas stations; the power of the Holy Spirit within you, let's start our journey through this little dilemma we call behavior modification.

As I mentioned before, feel free to plug in any of your own vices, weaknesses, temptations or serial pitfalls. But for the purpose of a communal roadmap, I will focus on the over utilization of fermented grape juice. OK, we might as well call a spade a spade, which fits in rather well, especially if your vice may be gambling. For clarification, let's just define it as drinking too much wine, beer, vodka, gin, scotch, rum, tequila and all those other "spirits" one may obtain at that other "spirit shop". My apologies if I missed your drink of choice, as I just listed my past favorites. The emphasis is on the past, thanks to the power of the Holy Spirit. I hope you have figured out by now that we are all in this thing called human nature together, no matter where your shortcomings may be found.

LEAVE ON SHELF:

You are not truly a Christian unless you can abide by the law: The Ten Commandments, within the realm of your own natural power. Nothing could be further from the truth, as this is a man-made belief.

ADD TO CART:

The power of the Holy Spirit is a gift of grace and mercy from Jesus Christ, who died for your salvation and righteousness.

Perhaps one of the most heart-breaking situations we experience as Christians is the failure to call upon the power of the Holy Spirit when faced with a temptation of the flesh. And when we choose to enter this turmoil, armed with anything other than the Holy Spirit, we always experience the same results. This defeat is magnified by the fact that our "fall from grace" is often witnessed by those who are closest to us. Our concern for ourselves; or better yet, our anxiety in regard to our "Christian image" being damaged, actually gives us another sign that we are not only on the wrong track, but equipped with the wrong motives as well. Any time our walk with Christ is focused on the observation of others, we can rest assured we have strayed from the Holy Spirit's directed course. Christ even tells us in *Matthew 6:1 (NIV)*: *"Be careful not to do your 'acts of righteousness' before men, to be seen by them. If you do, you will have no reward from your Father in heaven."* If our first concern when faced with defeat is for our own image, then we have not only missed the mark, but soon discover we are not even in the right arena.

After a few of these, and normally it occurs after the second failure; due to the fact that most people will give you a second chance, we soon throw in the towel. We walk away, head down, returning to more comfortable surroundings. The comfortable surroundings in this instance are a sustained quagmire of life within the natural spirit. We may even be greeted by salutations such as: "Good to see you again," or "I feel like I have an old friend back again." The sad news here is the reality that the welcome mat being extended has your footprints already on it. And these footprints result from you having wiped your shoes after walking through the mud; making your way back from the Holy Spirit.

The heartbreak that occurs from these defeats is not really within our hearts. Sure, we may be a little downtrodden for a season, but human nature has a way of patching this up in very short order. And as we venture further and further into the darkness of this human nature, we soon discover that we are immune to our iniquities, if in fact we give much thought to it at all.

The real heartbreak occurs within the heart of Christ, but probably not for the reasons you would first assume. Christ is not heartbroken from your failure, as he will never give up on you. He will continue to pursue you through the Holy Spirit's beckoning. But the heartbreaker resides in the fact that we consider this "fall from grace" to actually be a fall from grace at all. I apologize for setting you up for this one earlier, but you may have noticed that I did place the words: "fall from grace" in quotation marks. In this case, the quotation marks emphasize the fact that once we have accepted Christ as our Savior, baptized in the Holy Spirit as a result of this acceptance through our faith, there is no such thing as a "fall from grace." Christ is heartbroken because we have placed a superficial limit on his abundant and eternal mercy, and the grace he continually offers.

We are ashamed to come back, but this shame is never originating from the Holy Spirit. This shame is driven by the natural spirits of this world, appealing to your human nature. They are placing a false limit on God's grace and mercy. The welcome mat you have just walked across when you returned to your old haunts or spirits in this case, never replaces the "Red-Carpet" God has eternally extended to you: *Revelation 19:13 (NIV): He is dressed in a robe dipped in blood, and his name is the Word of God.* This robe is dipped in the blood of salvation, and extended to each and every one of us with a grace that is eternal, through the sacrifice of God's Son: Jesus Christ.

PRAYER POINT:

I praise the Father for the gifts of eternal salvation through the Son and abundant life within the Holy Spirit. I give thanksgiving to the Father for his grace that knows no end.

AISLE FIVE
The Playing Field

I have underestimated the cost of my own effort. The enemy's strength and numbers are inconceivable.

Psalm 44:3 (NIV): It was not by their sword that they won the land, nor did their arm bring them victory; it was your right hand, your arm, and the light of your face, for you loved them.

Proverbs 23: 29-35 (NIV): Who has woe? Who has sorrow? Who has strife? Who has complaints? Who has needless bruises? Who has blood-shot eyes? Those who linger over wine, who sample bowls of mixed wine. Do not gaze at wine when it is red, when it sparkles in the cup, when it goes down smoothly! In the end it bites like a snake and poisons like a viper. Your eyes will see strange sights and your mind imagine confusing things. You will be like one sleeping on the high seas, lying on top of the rigging. "They hit me," you will say, "but I am not hurt! They beat me, but I don't feel it! When will I wake up so I can find another drink?"

Now, don't start thinking I am pointing the all high and mighty finger exclusively at you here. This reminds me of the numerous times yours truly fell off the wagon while attempting to drive this little team of wild horses by my own strength and willpower.

You have to admit that *Proverbs 23: 29-35* does sound a little bit like a hangover morning or perhaps a rude awakening after any kind of slip, especially considering it may have come at the end of a long string of successful abstinence that you have managed to accumulate by sheer determination and grit. To make matters worse, this momentary carnal success was amid the praise and reinforcement of well meaning friends and family, where "you can do this" or "you look great," have now ended in another defeat. Even though your first concern is not what others may think, regretfully, once again, you are reminded that the beast was not really dead, but was only sleeping.

Do you get the feeling as you continually approach this battle from a position of natural strength that you may not be on a level playing field? That's because you're not! Paul outlines just what we are up against in *Ephesians 6:12 (NIV)*: *"For our struggle is not against flesh and blood, but against the rulers, against the authorities, against the powers of this dark world and against the spiritual forces of evil in the heavenly realms."* Think about it! You are attempting to do combat with supernatural forces by utilizing your own means. And to make matters worse, you are defaulting to your fragile willpower when you possess the very power that will defeat these forces of darkness every time: the Holy Spirit.

Granted, you may be able to win one every once in a while, but at the end of the day these are not even battles. These are simply small skirmishes in a war for your life; the life God created you to live. At the end of the day you are losing not only the battle, but the war itself. You will soon discover that this fight, fueled by your own strength or lack there-of, often provides you with just enough success at just the right time to keep you throwing the dice. OK, there I go with the gambling again, but as I explained before; feel free to plug in your own vices, as the Holy Spirit is a non-discriminatory healer. *Jeremiah 33:6 (NIV): Nevertheless, I will bring health and healing to it. I will heal my people and will let them enjoy abundant peace and security.* It is also no coincidence when relying on your own strength and determination that you soon find yourself participating in a hopeless dance, a frustrating "Three Step" if you will: One step forward and two steps back.

Christ describes this "Three Step" in *Matthew 12: 43-45 (NIV)*: *"When an evil spirit comes out of a man, it goes through arid places seeking rest and does not find it. Then, it says, 'I will return to the house I left.' When it arrives it finds the house unoccupied, swept clean and put in order, then it goes and takes with it seven other spirits more wicked than itself, and they go in and live there. And the final condition of that man is worse than the first. That is how it will be with this wicked generation."* So the moral of this demonic possession story is simply that being your own exorcist without the power of the Holy Spirit will eventually leave you worse off than you were before. The natural spirit, the character of man, woman's natural strength or whatever you choose to name it, simply will not cut it long term.

By now I think you will agree with the uneven playing field Paul outlines in Ephesians 6, where both end zones appear to have the home team's logo firmly stamped on this "artificial" turf: SINFUL NATURE. And you thought this was going to be a neutral site. No, my friend, there are quite a bit more forces in play here than what meets the eye. The enemies that ally themselves with sinful nature are rarely visible, and the beast is perfectly able to wage consistent war even with eyes closed.

If you truly examine the times you have overindulged, partaking of the wrong spirit; you will discover that drinking to excess or any other overindulgence is a default reaction to temporarily overcome the emptiness you are experiencing from this sinful nature. This state of mind or sinful nature is usually a result of your spirit being D.E.A.D. Yes, pardon the acronym, but "spirit overindulgence" is typically a reaction to: Despair (losing hope and confidence), Envy (a resentment of someone that has something you want), Anxiety (an unpleasant state of turmoil, worry or apprehension) and Discouragement (loss of confidence or enthusiasm). It is imperative during these D.E.A.D. spiritual times that we default to life in the Spirit. Or in this case, the one that gives the Spirit: *John 10:10 (NIV): The thief comes only to steal and kill, and destroy; I have come that they may have life and have it to the full.* Don't let the thief steal your joy with the smoke and mirrors of a D.E.A.D. spirit.

Proverbs 6: 16-19 (NIV) gives us six things the Lord hates and seven that are detestable to him. The big seven are *haughty eyes* (pride), *a lying tongue, hands that shed innocent blood* (I am quite sure this is literally and figuratively), *a heart that devises wicked schemes, feet that are quick to rush into evil, a false witness who pours out lies and a person who stirs up conflict within the community.* I believe you will agree that this list is basically synonymous with the list Paul outlines in *Galatians 5:19.* So it becomes imperative that you call upon the Holy Spirit to help you recognize the edge of the cliff. You need to call upon the Holy Spirit to substitute the fruits of the Spirit: love, joy, peace, patience, kindness, goodness, faithfulness, gentleness and self control. This needs to occur before you reach for that second or third spirit; or for some of us: the first.

It is very interesting that "*haughty eyes*" or pride is the first bad behavior listed in *Proverbs 6:16.* This is no coincidence, due to the fact that pride was the first act of the sinful nature against the Holy Spirit in the Garden of Eden. If you read *Genesis 3,* you will find that the serpent tempted Eve by appealing to her pride. In other words, the serpent told Eve that if she ate the forbidden fruit she would not surely die and as a matter of fact she would become like God. Her pride drove her to eat the fruit so that she could be an equal to God, at least in her viewpoint. One certainly cannot let Adam off the "haughty eye" hook either. Adam arrives on the scene seconds later and makes the same choice. Adam's choice is based on pride as well. Adam makes this choice so that Eve would not get too far ahead of him in the human pecking order. In other words, Adam's pride enabled him to choose an ill-fated spirit over obedience to God, and he lost paradise on earth in the bargain. This was the initial proof of *Proverbs 16:18 (NIV): Pride goes before destruction, a haughty spirit before a fall.*

So when we are tempted to set ourselves up to replace God's Spirit with our own "haughty spirit," and then soon fail as we will always do when we make this tradeoff; the default reaction is to wash away the shame with a kindred natural or evil spirit. But how do we avoid this? I mean, from firsthand experience, this can sneak up on you in the dark side of the old neighborhood bar and grill. So how do we just "magically" interchange this natural spirit for the fruits of the Spirit?

Thankfully, Paul does not abandon us to our own weak devices as he presents us with our own brand new uniforms and equipment in *Ephesians 6: 17-18 (NIV): "Take the helmet of salvation and the sword of the Spirit, which is the word of God. And Pray in the Spirit on all occasions with all kinds of prayers and requests."* We do battle with these forces of the sinful nature by utilizing a game plan which has two plays. Fortunately this is all we will ever need to achieve victory time and time again; if we will only access them. First, we acknowledge (helmet = mind) in faith, that we are saved and made righteous in the eyes of God by the salvation of Christ, which is his sacrifice on the cross for our sins. Then, we need to realize that we have full and immediate access to the power of the Spirit through his Word; the Holy Bible and Christ. We must take advantage of this in order to defeat these opponents.

You are confirming the fact that God made you in his image, as God called upon Christ and the Holy Spirit to create mankind in the beginning: *Genesis 1:26 (NIV): Then God said, "Let us make man in our image, in our likeness, and let him rule over the fish of the sea and the birds of the air, over the livestock, over all earth and over all the creatures that move along the ground."* I particularly like the part of man's dominance over "*all creatures that move along the ground.*" It serves as a not so gentle reminder that we possess the power through the Holy Spirit to "trample" on the serpent

(Satan). We are empowered to do this because we are created in God's image, which surely includes God's Spirit within us.

The acknowledgment of our salvation and the act of accessing the power of the Holy Spirit through God's word are actually acts of worship. And through these acts we fortify our strength within the Holy Spirit: *John 4: 23-24 (NIV): Yet a time is coming and has now come when the true worshippers will worship the Father in spirit and in truth, for they are the kind of worshippers the Father seeks. God is spirit, and his worshippers must worship in spirit and in truth.*

In regard to that playing field; the glory of living in the Spirit and the luxury of calling on the Spirit's power is the fact that it comes through the One that can not only change your drinking habits, but also adds abundance and joy to life: *Psalm 16: 5-6 (NIV): Lord, you have assigned me my portion and my cup; you have made my lot secure. The boundary lines have fallen for me in pleasant places.* Jesus also describes the ultimate "beverage of choice" to the Samaritan woman at the well in *John 4: 13-14 (NIV): Jesus answered, "Everyone who drinks this water will be thirsty again, but whoever drinks the water I give him will never thirst. Indeed, the water I give him will become in him a spring of water welling up to eternal life."*

LEAVE ON SHELF:

It is crucial that you dismiss the false perception that you only have to ask one time. Asking for spiritual reinforcement through acknowledgment of the Holy Spirit's power within you requires a daily vigilance, if not moment to moment for some days.

ADD TO CART:

You are not on a level playing field when left to your own devices and strength.

I remember attending a support group meeting for substance abuse several years ago. It was not Alcoholics Anonymous, even though I highly recommend that organization to anyone who is struggling with this disease. I was sitting with a friend of mine, who was attending that meeting to fulfill a court order on a DUI conviction. And yes, this is serious stuff we are dealing with here, which can often go very wrong; real quick. There was another gentleman sharing (talking) across the room; who was also in attendance due to a mandatory invitation. I will call the gentleman who was talking "Bobby" for the sake of anonymity. My friend sitting next to me, who had multiple issues very similar to mine, leaned over and whispered: "I'll bet you 10 to 1, Bobby doesn't make it."

I have to admit, it was ironically funny at the time. I mean, here we are sitting in a meeting for substance abuse, with two of the three of us in attendance by demand, and one vice "plays" off of the other in an innocence so subdued, it was barely recognizable.

I could stop there, leaving you with a bit of a light hearted smile when you consider the multiple complications of this unlevel playing field we call human nature. But I need to tell you that I am the only surviving member of this story. Bobby and my friend both passed away too early; my friend with lung cancer (a habitual smoker) and Bobby with liver and kidney failure.

I have missed them both, even though I know I will see them again. I am assured of this because I witnessed to both of them over the years, and know for a fact they both accepted Christ as their Savior. I am sometimes haunted by that witness however, because they both often "witnessed" my personal failures due to my reliance upon my own strength and willpower. But I rest in the mercy of Christ, as he grants us eternal forgiveness, no matter what side of the playing field we find our witness: *John 15: 4-5 (NIV): Remain in me, and I will remain in you. No branch can bear fruit by itself; it must remain in the vine. Neither can you bear fruit unless you remain in me. I am the vine; you are the branches. If a man remains in me and I in him, he will bear much fruit; apart from me you can do nothing.* And I thank God for the times he has granted me the wisdom to call upon the Holy Spirit, and therefore "remain in him," rather than facing these demons on my own lack of accord.

"The Lord only knows," as we say here on earth, that once you consider the demonic roster the home team places on the artificial turf both in Paul's day and ours, that the conversation which takes place between Christ and the demon-possessed man in *Luke 8 (NIV)* comes as no surprise: *Luke 8: 29-31 (NIV): For Jesus had commanded the evil spirit to come out of the man. Many times it had seized him, and though he was chained hand and foot and kept under guard, he had broken his chains and had been driven by the demon into solitary places. Jesus asked him, "What is your name?" "Legion," he replied, because many demons had gone into him.* The "Legion" team roster, today and yesterday, looks a little like this: pride, psychics, smoking, drinking to excess, gambling, pride, witchcraft, sexual immorality, impurity, pride, debauchery, hatred, pride, discord, dissensions, horoscopes, pride, fits of rage, road rage, selfish ambition, workaholic, pride, envy, orgies, pornography, some television, most movies, jealousy, gluttony, pride, a lying tongue, hands that shed innocent blood and feet that are quick to rush into evil, and last but not least; did I mention pride? But the good news here is the fact that the Holy Spirit has you covered, no matter how many angles these demonic angels may take. Yes, the Holy Spirit is the ultimate insurance agent. And in this particular case you do receive both "term / abundant" and "whole / eternal" life policies.

I would be remiss if I did not tell you that God's angels; the "good guys," are also here with us on this earthly sphere we mistakenly call our home. Michael and Gabriel are the two angels of God that are mentioned in the Bible. Gabriel appears to be in charge of announcements, as he was the one that explained to Mary that she would give birth to Jesus. Gabriel was also the one who told Zechariah that his wife

Elizabeth would bear him a son and his name was to be John. You will probably remember him as John the Baptist, and Gabriel even left specific instructions as to John's abstinence: *Luke 1: 14-16 (NIV): He will be a joy and delight to you, and many will rejoice because of his birth, for he will be great in the sight of the Lord. He is never to take wine or other fermented drink, and he will be filled with the Holy Spirit even from birth. Many of the people of Israel will he bring back to the Lord their God.*

As I told you earlier, Bobby "didn't make it" and I had the honor of officiating at his funeral. I would like to share a little something that happened at that funeral.

"We needed you down here today and you came through for us." Those were the words of the late sixties rather portly gentleman in the ill-fitted suit and uneven tie, sitting off to the side of the buffet table at the funeral reception. He caught me somewhat by surprise, due to the fact that I had not remembered seeing him in the small congregation moments earlier within the dimly lit funeral home chapel. "Where do you call home?" he continued. And before I could acknowledge his compliment, as I continued to work my way down the buffet, carefully selecting my dessert along with my reply, Bobby's mother approached me and thanked me for my kind words.

When I turned to readdress the stranger, he was nowhere to be found, even upon my further inquiries and descriptions given to the small group of family and friends that day. "We needed you down here today," first appeared to be a geographical preface, because we made the trip from Oklahoma City down to Dallas. But the question that followed the compliment will always lead me to believe that any answer I could have offered him would have been rhetorical at best: "Where do you call home?"

Hebrews 13: 1-2 (NIV): Keep on loving each other as brothers. Do not forget to entertain strangers, for by so doing some people have entertained angels without knowing it. You are probably wondering if the stranger was an angel or just a product of a vivid imagination. Well, I will let you decide. But I will remind you that we were at Bobby's funeral that day, which marked the beginning of his first real freedom from many of our mutual addictions. And by the way, the verse that directly follows this little notice about angels dwelling here on earth may help you decide: *Hebrews 13: 3 (NIV): Remember those in prison as if you were their fellow prisoners, and those who are mistreated as if you yourselves were suffering.*

And until I do finally arrive at the place I can truly call my home, I will rest in the assurance of *Psalm 91:11-15 (NIV): For he will command his angels concerning you to guard you in all your ways; they will lift you up in their hands, so that you will not strike your foot against a stone. You will tread upon the lion and the serpent. "Because he loves me," says the Lord, "I will rescue him; I will protect him, for he acknowledges my name. He will call upon me, and I will answer him; I will be with him in trouble, I will deliver him and honor him."*

"We needed you down here today, and you came through for us." And until I arrive at that destination, the place I will truly "call home," I will take the stranger's kind words, not so much as a compliment, but a marching order for all of the ones like Bobby that God places in my life along the way: *Luke 23:43 (NIV): Jesus answered him, "I tell you the truth, today you will be with me in paradise."*

PRAYER POINT:

In remembrance of the Son's sacrifice, and now through my faith, I call upon the Holy Spirit for my daily power and strength: *"Give us today, our daily bread" Matthew 6:11 (NIV).*

AISLE SIX

Four Swords

**My willpower and courage to fight begin to give way.
Creature comforts and pipedreams of temporary asylum are
rapidly exhausting the remains of my arsenal.**

*Psalm 20:7 (NIV): Some trust in chariots and some trust in horses, but
we trust in the name of the Lord our God.*

"*D*o not get drunk on wine, which leads to debauchery. Instead be filled
with the Holy Spirit." *Ephesians 5:18 (NIV)*

Were the words "easier said than done" ever so appropriate? If you
have struggled with any addiction, you soon learn that catch phrases
such as: "failure is not an option" or "God helps those who help themselves," are plastic swords when the dragon begins to stir. While I believe
it was certainly a wonderful campaign that did a lot of good; "Just Say
No," is only a fragile beginning, without the ultimate power of the Holy
Spirit. When the beast or dragon awakens within you, it is crucial to access the power within; to fight fire with fire.

If you remember Aisle Two or perhaps you may want to refer to the
"original text": *Genesis 1:1-4*, where God, the Word (Jesus Christ) and
the Spirit, were all present "*In the beginning*," and God said, "*Let there be*

light": God, the Father, spoke creation into existence through the Power (Spirit) of his Word (Christ). There is an unfathomable power available to us through God's Word. That power manifests itself within our inner being through the sacrifice of Christ, who has given us the Holy Spirit. Therefore, to seek any other means to combat an enemy when we cannot see or assess its total power is incomprehensible; if we ever desire a life changing victory like the Almighty God may exclusively provide.

So, in case you haven't nailed it down so far, let me come right out and say it. We access the power of the Spirit (which Christ gave us through his sacrifice on the cross), by drawing on the Word of the Lord: Christ and the Scripture; the Righteousness and the Word of God. The "Word of God" is the Sword of the Spirit. The prophet Isaiah tells us of the benefits of accessing and speaking God's word back to him in prayer and the power which is available to us within the Word: *Isaiah 55: 8-11 (NIV)*: "*For my thoughts are not your thoughts, neither are your ways my ways," declares the Lord. "As the heavens are higher than the earth, so are my ways higher than your ways and my thoughts than your thoughts. As the rain and the snow come down from heaven, and do not return to it without watering the earth and making it bud and flourish, so that it yields seed for the sower and bread for the eater, so is my word that goes out from my mouth: It will not return to me empty, but will accomplish what I desire and achieve the purpose for which I sent it.*"

The uneven playing field that Paul describes in *Ephesians 6* mandates these marching orders from Isaiah. We are to arm ourselves with God's Scripture and use it like a sword (Sword of the Spirit) to fight temptation. Praying and meditating through the Spirit, utilizing the Word of God (The Scripture) is the only effective weapon we have in our arsenal. But thanks to God, this is the only one we will ever need. To put it in terms so simple a child could understand it: "It works every time." That is "every time" we rely on the Holy Spirit as true children of God, rather than believing we are all "grown up" and letting our pride mandate the use of our own willpower. To this end, I would like to recommend these four swords:

Sword #1: *"No, in all things we are more than conquerors through him who loved us: For I am convinced that neither death nor life, neither angels or demons, neither the present nor the future, nor any powers, neither height nor depth, nor anything else in all creation, will be able to separate us from the love of God that is in Christ Jesus our Lord." Romans 8: 37-39 (NIV)*

You are claiming a victory through faith by speaking God's word. You are acknowledging the victory and subsequent power of the Spirit that Christ has afforded you through his love and sacrifice on the cross for your sins, and then projecting that victorious power against the forces of demons, other powers of creation and the present and future challenges. You may have noticed this particular scripture in *Romans 8* begins with the word: "No", which is always a good starting point when resisting temptation. But this answer only works if the abundantly evil question: "Why not?" is answered exclusively by the power of the Holy Spirit within you. And the Holy Spirit's answer always includes collateral blessings: *Psalm 103:1-5 (NIV): Praise the Lord, O my soul; all my inmost being, praise his holy name. Praise the Lord, O my soul, and forget not all his benefits— who forgives all your sins and heals all your diseases, who redeems your life from the pit and crowns you with love and compassion, who satisfies your desires with good things so that your youth is renewed like the eagle's.*

Sword #2: *"I pray that out of his glorious riches, he may strengthen you with power through his Spirit in your inner being." Ephesians 3:16 (NIV)*

You are reaffirming the fact that God, through Christ (*his glorious riches*), has strengthened you with the power of the Holy Spirit and confirming the source of that power.

Sword #3: *"Teach me to do your will, for you are my God; may your good Spirit lead me on level ground." Psalm 143: 10 (NIV)*

The only reason you are no longer on a level playing field here is the fact that you now have a distinct advantage through the power of the

Holy Spirit. Through this power; the field, the day and your very own life are yours once again.

Sword #4: *"Create in me a pure heart, O God, and renew a steadfast spirit within me. Do not cast me from your presence or take your Holy Spirit from me. Restore to me the joy of your salvation and grant me a willing spirit to sustain me." Psalm 51: 10-12 (NIV)*

Perhaps my favorite sword, this Scripture has it all. You are asking God to create a pure heart within you and to reinforce your spirit by accessing his Spirit and the presence of Christ in your heart. You are asking for this battle to become a transformation to joy and peace. You are confirming the victory while reiterating your eternal need for his Spirit to win the battle. You are asking for the power of his Spirit to sustain your own spirit. The fact that the Psalmist asks for *"a willing spirit to sustain me,"* specifically the word *"sustain,"* tells us that this will need to be a repetitious request. *"My word will not return to me empty,"* as God states in *Isaiah 55 (NIV)*, is not a one-time final solution, but an invitation to eternal and consistent prayer, utilizing the Holy Bible; the Word of God.

LEAVE ON SHELF:

To continue asking for what God has already given demonstrates a lack of faith. In a word: False!

ADD TO CART:

We need to call upon the power of God's Holy Spirit through our faith in Christ Jesus, as we access the Word of God: The Holy Bible.

Christ tells us that we have to change and become like children in order to enter the kingdom of heaven: *(Matthew 18:3 NIV)*. In order to do this correctly, you have to be elementary in your approach. And in this case, we need to define "elementary" in several different ways.

First of all, I want to take you back to elementary school or grade school Sunday school classes if you were lucky enough to attend one. In the First Baptist Church Sunday school third grade class of 1963, and believe me this was a lot more fun than it sounds, we were called upon to memorize Scripture. For those of you who did not go to church, you will need to relate this to memorizing spelling words for the dreaded spelling test, which in our educational institution took place every Friday. The spelling test made Friday anything but casual. And the only religious experience, outside of praying that you would pass, was the fried fish squares the cafeteria served because the Catholics had to eat it. Either way; church or state, one needed to employ these elementary forms of education in memorization in order to receive a Sunday school class gold star or be permitted to enter fourth grade the following fall.

While the Sunday school class gold stars soon became a goal too lofty, with Susan Bumgardner so far ahead of the rest of us by the second month the entire situation was hopeless, the third grade spelling tests was a different animal. You see, the third grade spelling test, with the pass to fourth grade hanging in the balance, was quite simply a matter of life and death. This realization was elementary, and it is amazing how fast one may retain knowledge when the perception of survival within the real world is riding on it. However, the further one climbs up that ladder of life with issues of life and death hanging in the balance, where spelling words and the Word of God are in play; the latter is what will take you to the promised land, while the former simply enables you to appear really old while texting.

Grade school Sunday school classes were also a fantastic introduction to the Holy Bible, the Word of God, for any boy with thoughts of sword fights and battles dominating his imagination. And just in case you have lost your innocence along the way, perhaps with too many spelling tests, I might remind you this was still during the time that you also hated girls for the most part. So with my apologies to Susan

Bumgardner, wherever she may be today, I would direct your attention to books of the Old Testament such as Joshua; complete with swords, spears, opposing armies and the Battle of Jericho. And before you accuse me of leaving the ladies out; take a look at Judge Deborah in the book of *Judges* or perhaps Queen Esther, who saved the entire Jewish race in the book named after her: *Esther.*

Did I mention swords? Yes, the Holy Spirit has provided you with a few "Real Swords," within the Book of Joshua, which help us wage war against the opposing powers of today's real world, whenever and wherever they may be found:

Joshua 1: 3 (NIV): I will give you every place where you set your foot. This Scripture is a guarantee of victory, with one simple stipulation. "*Set your foot,*" in this case, means where you brace yourself and prepare for battle. And in this instance, the battle for abundant life takes place where you happen to find yourself this very day. "*Set your foot,*" means to ground yourself within the power of the Holy Spirit through God's Word.

Joshua 1: 7-9 (NIV): Be strong and very courageous. Be careful to obey all the law my servant Moses gave you; do not turn from it to the right or to the left, that you may be successful wherever you go. Do not let this Book of the Law depart from our mouth; meditate on it day and night, so that you may be careful to do everything written in it. Then you will be prosperous and successful. Have I not commanded you, be strong and courageous. Do not be terrified; do not be discouraged, for the Lord your God will be with you wherever you go. Now for some of you it would appear this Scripture with the directive to follow the law and to obey all of the law may have placed us back in the "struggling willpower category," where we have to do this with all of "our might."

But Christ gave us the Holy Spirit, who fights not only by our side, but is always out in front as well as covering our rear flank. Whenever the Bible gives you a directive, it is crucial that you accept it with the marching orders from the Holy Spirit's power and illuminating wisdom, once we have engaged the light of the Holy Spirit. You must have the Holy Spirit, the ultimate educational gift from Christ. Christ tells us the exact same thing, right after several elementary parables in *Luke: 8:16-18 (NIV)*: *"No one lights a lamp and hides it in a jar or puts it under a bed. Instead, he puts it on a stand, so that those who come in can see the light. For there is nothing hidden that will not be disclosed, and nothing concealed that will not be known or brought out into the open. Therefore, consider carefully how you listen. Whoever has will be given more; and whoever does not have, even what he thinks he has will be taken from him."* Quite simply, the Holy Spirit is your light, and it is through the power of that light within you that you are able to fulfill your true purpose in life. And that my friend is the ultimate v-i-c-t-o-r-y within the Holy Spirit, no matter how you spell it.

PRAYER POINT:

Give me the insight to call upon the power of the Holy Spirit, moment by moment, when daily petitions are not adequate; humbling my own natural strength like a child yields to the Father: *Psalm 119:11 (NIV): I have hidden your word in my heart, that I might not sin against you.*

AISLE SEVEN

Mocking spirits

I long to be transformed: to exorcise pride and showmanship for faith and hope.

Ezekiel 37:23 (NIV): They will no longer defile themselves with idols and vile images or with any of their offenses, for I will save them from all their sinful backsliding, and I will cleanse them. They will be my people and I will be their God.

❦

"*Do not be deceived: God cannot be mocked. A man reaps what he sows. The one who sows to please his sinful nature, from that nature will reap destruction; the one who sows to please the Spirit, from the Spirit will reap eternal life.*" Galatians 6: 7-8 (NIV)

I remember my older sister appealing to my mother, who was always judge and jury: "Mom! He's mocking me." I have to admit that I had to ask for a definition, the first time I heard this accusation. My mother's simple, yet sufficient reply was: "You are making fun of her by repeating what she says and does, when you really do not mean it." Cynical imitation or shallow mimicking may be better definitions, but the moral lesson probably would have been lost among the other "big words." Remember our goal here is to become like a child.

While it is true; as the old saying goes: "Imitation is the greatest form of flattery," hollow and false imitations are probably on the opposite end of the spectrum. We mock God when we hold ourselves out to be believers, but our actions, lifestyle and agendas portray a different story. Sometimes the imitations can be quite convincing as the world perceives them. God is never fooled, even though some of the greatest performances take place in the church. Christ painted a definition of it for the Pharisees in *Matthew 23:27-28 (NIV): "Woe to you, teachers of the law and Pharisees, you hypocrites! You are like whitewashed tombs, which look beautiful on the outside; but on the inside are full of dead men's bones and everything unclean. In the same way, on the outside you appear to people as righteous but on the inside you are full of hypocrisy and wickedness."*

Christ was actually telling them they had no spirit. They masqueraded as followers of the law, righteous to the blind eye, but only for show. Their hearts were not truly in it because they not only failed to acknowledge the love of God, but they were mocking the wisdom of the Spirit by substituting their own perceived knowledge. The love of God was the very "Spirit" of this law they were attempting to enforce by their own show of false strength. And Jesus lets them know about it too, in *Luke 11:52 (NIV): "Woe to you experts in the law, because you have taken away the key to knowledge. You yourselves have not entered, and you have hindered those who were entering."* The emphasis was definitely on the show as these hypocritical religious leaders walked around with Scriptures in little boxes; affixed to their hats and heads.

They were a sad bunch. In the case of these religious squares the term "misery loves company" was never so fitting. We often witness the same pious nature today when our behavior is questioned by some religious "character" that never seems to possess so much as a trace of joy or love. They were perfectly content to grind it out on their own, as they were imitating the law and mocking God at the same time. The Pharisees had the proverbial cart before the horse, the law and the attempted effort to follow the law by one's own means, before the Spirit and the power that accompany it. They lacked the true joy and love of Christ, which empowers the Spirit within to offer sincere love for our fellow man, and therefore enables one to "sow to please the Spirit."

Yes, "*God cannot be mocked,*" not after he has given us the gift of his Son and the power of the Holy Spirit. It is interesting to note that the last time he actually permitted "*mocking*" was right before Christ went to the Cross of Calvary, followed by his eventual resurrection and gift of the Spirit: *Matthew 27:31(NIV): After they had mocked him, they took off the robe and put his own clothes on him. Then they led him off to be crucified.*" So consider yourself "growing" in the Spirit, and part of that transition is to stop false imitations of what you want to be when you grow up.

The simple fact of the matter is that there is only room for One Spirit in your heart. God will not be a joint tenant. *Proverbs 20:1 (NIV): "Wine is a mocker and beer is a brawler; whoever is led astray by them is not wise."* Now, wait just a minute! Before we proceed, let me answer that question that is lingering in the back of your mind: "What's wrong with a glass of wine or a beer now and then?" While I will address that in further detail on Aisle Nine, the answer for the time being is: nothing; for some folks that is. However, I firmly believe the key phrase in *Proverbs 20* is: "*led astray*"; as in seeking another entity to fill the void, the emptiness which can only be filled by the Spirit of God. God has even placed this desire to fill the emptiness within our hearts. *Ecclesiastes 3: 10-11(NIV): "I have seen the burden God has laid on men. He has made everything beautiful in its time. He has also set eternity in the hearts of men; yet they cannot fathom what God has done from beginning to end."* The Scripture; "*set eternity in the hearts of men,*" actually means that God has implanted a desire within your heart and an emptiness within you, that may only be fulfilled by the acceptance of his Son Jesus Christ as your personal Savior. This acceptance by faith consequently enables you to become one in the Spirit with God, which is the only genuine and lasting way to fulfill this void. You will not be able to satisfy this spiritual abyss by reaching for one too many. You will find yourself to be like the little boy with his finger in the dam, and the minute you remove it the hole just gets worse. And for those of you that are still hung up on the moderation issue, I believe if beer makes you a brawler, you may be "mocking" moderation.

LEAVE ON SHELF:

Mocking spirits that offer a demeaning and temporary comfort, monopolizing the heart with wrong motives that always end in failure, fear and destruction need to be left in the past.

ADD TO CART:

Sincerely pursue and access the One True Spirit with all your mind and soul, from the love of Christ within you, building your house on the solid ground of the Holy Spirit.

Matthew 7: 26-27 (NIV): But everyone who hears these words of mine and does not put them into practice is like a foolish man who built his house on sand. The rain came down, the streams rose, and the winds blew and beat against that house, and it fell with a great crash.

I watched from my fortress of sand and shells as he walked towards the surf. This was my father, a man who was larger than life. Even though it has been a lifetime since that day, the memory still lingers. This was the first unguarded moment when a child senses a chink in the armor, a crack in the fortress wall that shed the first light of doubt. This led me to believe that this man may be as fragile as the sanctuaries we built on those shores; the castles of sand and shells. Upon returning to the beach the next day, gravitating towards that same piece of driftwood that anchored the highest tower of the castle, one soon discovered that these earthly kingdoms had washed away.

Vacations at the beach were always a time to relax, to let go, and for most of the time in my father's case, to have one too many. He was a man of great character, an honest Christian man, an attorney by trade, and a son of a Baptist minister. Therefore, the legacy always seemed appropriate; where leisure time transitioned into excess for me as well, when I found myself under that same summer sun years later.

I will always revere my father and his words often come back to me today, like seashells washed in by the tide. Some are perfectly formed, though some are partial and tattered. I wonder now, just how his same mistakes could have become mine. He knew the Word of God and had long since placed his fate in the hands of Christ our Savior. But at the end of the day he was his own man, at least by self perception, and chose to cross those waters on his accord alone. And even though I will continue to imitate his spirit in so many ways, I will not turn away the only One who truly offers us the power to navigate life's seas: *Luke 11: 11-13 (NIV): "Which of you fathers, if your son asks for a fish, will give him a snake instead? Or if he asks for an egg, will give him a scorpion? If you then, though you are evil, know how to give good gifts to your children, how much more will your Father in heaven give the Holy Spirit to those who ask him!"*

PRAYER POINT:

Grant me the wisdom to pursue the Holy Spirit, thereby obtaining the courage to dismiss hollow substitutes.

AISLE EIGHT

Asking

How many times have I searched the darkness in vain for that first glimmer of hope that arrives with the dawn?

Isaiah 21: 11-12 (NIV): "Watchman, what is left of the night? Watchman, what is left of the night?" The watchman replies, "Morning is coming but also the night. If you would ask, then ask; and come back yet again."

If you find that you are tired of failing or just plain worn out by the constant struggle to maintain this lifestyle that appears to only work for those people that you are not so sure you want to associate with anyway, and quest after quest to achieve this holy grail have resulted in utter failure, here is the one word that will change your life: Ask!

It really cannot be that simple, right? Unfortunately, you are correct, due to the fact that the caveat that always accompanies this little three letter word is to ask in confidence and ask in faith. Ask, while knowing Christ will answer. He will answer because you have accepted his saving grace and mercy through your belief in his death on the cross and his resurrection that makes you righteous in the eyes of God. If you are ready for the short version of that, Christ tells us in *Matthew 21:22 (NIV):*

"If you believe, you will receive whatever you ask for in prayer." If you require something with a little more effort on your part, Christ offers you this one, which is a little bit more labor intense: *Matthew 7:7 (NIV): "Ask and it will be given unto you; seek and you will find; knock and the door will be opened. For everyone who asks receives; he who seeks finds; and to him who knocks, the door will be opened."*

It is important to realize, that *Matthew 7:7* contains three verbs, and they all pertain to you: ask, seek and knock. I like to think of asking as the entry level, the introduction to the realization of what we have already received through our belief in Christ as our Savior. We are not so much asking for the Holy Spirit, because Christ baptized us in the Holy Spirit the moment we believed and accepted him as our Savior. We are asking for the acknowledgment and the application of that Spirit within our particular circumstances, so that we may draw upon this incredible power source, this abundance of fortified and reinforced willpower, where the impossible not only becomes a reality, but often arrives on the scene with relative ease.

Do not be afraid to be specific or ask for comfort, as there is no "law" against it. Ask God through the power of the Holy Spirit within you to "make it easy," to "lighten the burden." Ask God to replace your longing and desire with peace and joy; however you may define peace and joy in your particular set of circumstances. And the real beauty of "asking in the Spirit," is the fact that we may not even know what would give us peace and joy in our particular setting, but the Spirit knows, and that is all that matters. The expediency of your fortified willpower will be amazing, once you acknowledge the true source of that power: the Holy Spirit within you.

So many times, Jesus is simply waiting for us to ask. It is from the asking, when our faith is already engaged, that Christ is glorified. *Matthew 8: 2-3(NIV): A man with leprosy came and knelt before him and said, "Lord if you are willing, you can make me clean." Jesus reached out his hand and touched the man. "I am willing,"* he said, *"Be clean!"* The leper asked in faith, as he never doubted Christ could perform the miracle. *"Lord if you are willing, you can make me clean,"* is a sheer statement of faith in our case as well, because we may rest assured through God's Word, that it is truly the Lord's will to make you not only clean, but sober in this case.

Another instance of Christ waiting for us to ask is found in *Matthew 20: 29-34 (NIV): As Jesus and his disciples were leaving Jericho, a large crowd followed him. Two blind men were sitting by the roadside, and when they heard that Jesus was going by, they shouted, "Lord, Son of David, have mercy on us!" The crowd rebuked them and told them to be quiet, but they shouted all the louder, "Lord, Son of David, have mercy on us!" Jesus stopped and called them. "What do you want me to do for you?" he asked. "Lord," they answered, "we want our sight." Jesus had compassion on them and touched their eyes. Immediately they received their sight and followed him.* Yes, he is waiting for you to ask, even though he already knows what it is you want, as well as what it is you really need and when you need it. He even gives you this wisdom through the Holy Spirit's power within you.

Once we have asked, we then move on to the business of seeking, which is a practice in escalating power through faith; a type of fueling station for the Spirit within us. I do not honestly know of a better place to grow in the power of Christ and the Holy Spirit than the very Word of God: The Holy Bible. The following two Scriptures pertain to the Holy Spirit specifically, but rest assured if you *"seek"*, God will plug you into your own power sources with expedience and accuracy in regard to your individual circumstances.

Ezekiel 36: 25-27 (NIV): "I will sprinkle clean water on you, and you will be clean; I will cleanse you from all your impurities and from all your idols. I will give you a new heart and put a new spirit in you; I will remove from you your heart of flesh. And I will put my Spirit in you and move you to follow my decrees and be careful to keep my laws."

Be just as specific in your "seeking" as you were in your asking, discovering Scriptures that emphasize and magnify the power: "*And I will put my Spirit in you and move you to follow my decrees,*" tells me this is no longer mine alone to fight. But I have now called upon the only One that will be victorious. I believe that the "cleansing of all impurities" even covers elements that may be generating sins of excess which include the ones I may not even be aware of or suspect; pride, envy and idolatry. These three have a tendency to sneak up on me, be it ever so subtle.

John 14: 13-18 (NIV): "And I will do whatever you ask in my name, so that the Son may bring glory to the Father. You may ask me for anything in my name and I will do it. If you love me you will obey what I command. And I will ask the Father and he will give you another Counselor to be with you forever – the Spirit of truth. The world cannot accept him, because it neither sees him nor knows him. But you know him for he lives with you and will be in you."

The process of "seeking" is actually an exercise of letting God take control by enabling his Spirit to propel you. It is actually a very peaceful way to confront the demons of desire and the monsters of the flesh; because you are combating these supernatural spiritual forces for the first time with strength they do not have a chance of defeating. Pay particular attention to the qualification of "*in my name*" in this Scripture: "*ask me for anything in my name.*" To "ask in his name," actually means to ask within his will. This is where "seeking" enters the picture because God will reveal his "will" within his Word (The Holy Bible), and translate and define that to you through his Holy Spirit. The good news is that the will of God is for you to be sober, truthful, humble, joyful, loving, and at peace within any circumstance, and the Holy Spirit orchestrates this, if you will seek God's will through his instruction manual for life: The Holy Bible.

The bad news is the will of God may or may not include that new boat or mansion you had your heart set on, at least not on this side of paradise that is. However, at the risk of floundering, there is nothing in God's word that rules these items out for you either. So, in an attempt to not leave you marooned without a boat or without a house so big that the last three generations of your family could live in it, I would direct you to the business at hand. *Matthew 6: 31-33 (NIV): So do not worry, saying, 'What shall we eat?' or 'What shall we drink?' or 'What shall we wear?' For the pagans run after all these things and your heavenly Father knows that you need them. But seek first his kingdom and his righteousness, and all these things will be given to you as well. Therefore, do not worry about tomorrow, for tomorrow will worry about itself. Each day has enough trouble of its own.* Did you catch the last verse of that Scripture? This was the origin of "one day at a time." "Seeking his kingdom and his righteousness" begins with seeking his Word; Jesus Christ, and his gift of righteousness; the Holy Spirit, on a daily basis.

Last but certainly not least is the business of knocking. Knocking is certainly more physical than asking or seeking and this is where most of us make our mistakes. Now that we are reinforced by acknowledging the Holy Spirit's power within us (ask) and we have sought to strengthen that through the Word of God (seek), we now arrive at that proverbial door, where we are required to "knock." The last thing we want to do here; having asked for affirmation of the Spirit within, while continuing to seek God's Word, is to knock in the sense that we are once again taking action by our own accord. In this case, we do not want to charge off and attempt to knock the door in by our own strength. I like to think of knocking as a gentle acceptance of God's power through the Holy Spirit. This is actually an exercise in patience as we invite the Holy Spirit to consistently lead. Notice the term is "knocking" as opposed to "pounding or battering." There is always a certain degree of patience involved if we are to obtain a longstanding peace.

There is a verse in the Psalms that many people often misinterpret when it comes to the business of asking, seeking and knocking: *Psalm 37:4(NIV): "Delight yourself in the Lord, and he will give you the desires of your heart."* So many times people, including myself, have viewed this verse as a type of magic lamp when it comes to asking God for blessings. Usually, this A to Z list consists of items, agendas, and wishes that we perceive as essential to our happiness. We need to reverse the model and realize that when we live in the Spirit and the Spirit lives in us, we do in fact receive a *"new heart"* as stated earlier in *Ezekiel 36: 25-27 (NIV),* and God, through the Holy Spirit, actually changes what our hearts desire. God places new desires in your heart, enabling you to align with his will and word.

Revelation 3: 20-22 (NIV): "Here I am! I stand at the door and knock. If anyone hears my voice and opens the door, I will come in and eat with him and he with me. To him who overcomes, I will give the right to sit with me on my throne, just as I overcame and sat down with my Father on his throne. He who has an ear, let him hear what the Spirit says to the churches." And wouldn't you rather fight your battles from the throne of God, rather than out there on the streets by yourself?

Knocking, in this instance, is what I like to consider the beckoning of the Holy Spirit's gentle reminder that God will give us "new" desires, in his own beautiful time. We may then add to this, the additional bonus, as we receive a restful joy along the way, which outdistances the temporary happiness of this "stuff" we think we need. *Matthew 11:28-30(NIV): "Come to me, all you who are weary and burdened, and I will give you rest. Take my yoke upon you and learn from me, for I am gentle and humble in heart, and you will find rest for your souls. For my yoke is easy and my burden is light."* Knocking is similar to asking, as they both relate to prayer, but in the instance of knocking, we are actually praying in the Holy Spirit: *Jude 20 (NIV): "But you, dear friends, build yourselves up in your most holy faith and pray in the Holy Spirit."* Picture yourself as knocking on the door of your own heart in order to open your heart to the realization of the Holy Spirit's power. When I am reduced to the point of clinched hands from the limited strength of my own willpower, once again reaching the bitter end, I should gently tap on my own heart with those knuckles, like the knocking on a door; beckoning the Holy Spirit's entry.

Remember, that God has *"set eternity in the hearts of men"* (*Ecclesiastes 3:11 NIV*), and the fact that we now have the "fruit of the Spirit" within us, causes us to *"groan inwardly as we wait eagerly for our adoption as sons, the redemption of our bodies,"* as Paul tells us in *Romans 8:23 (NIV)*. When we "knock on our own hearts," and let the Holy Spirit take control, just as Jesus stands at the door and knocks, we are actually waiting in patience, taking a step back, and listening and observing in the peace that only the Holy Spirit will allow. Paul puts it very eloquently in *Romans 8: 26-27 (NIV)*, directly after he has just reminded us to "wait for it patiently" in *Romans 8:25 (NIV)*: *"In the same way, the Spirit helps us in our weakness. We do not know what we ought to pray for, but the Spirit himself intercedes for us with groans that words cannot express. And he who searches our hearts knows the mind of the Spirit, because the Spirit intercedes for the saints in accordance with God's will."* The beauty and the security of the Holy Spirit interceding on our behalf is the fact that we do not know where the ambush awaits, but the Spirit knows. Through that employment, the Holy Spirit has conquered before we even get there, waiting in hope, for us to acknowledge the miracle.

LEAVE ON SHELF:

We need to stop conducting general and redundant forms of prayer, simply out of a sense of obligation. We often throw these prayers on God's doorstep as we scurry off to conduct our busy lives, never bothering to wait for any kind of results or future direction.

ADD TO CART:

Ask God for the realization of the Holy Spirit, seek the Holy Spirit through his Word, and recognize the knock of the Holy Spirit on the door of your own heart, enabling the power of the Holy Spirit within you to change the desires of your heart.

"Open please," were some of the first words she ever said to me. This was Avery, my granddaughter, and I had just given her a bag of her favorite cookies. She knew exactly what they were and was even more aware that handing them back to me was the most expedient way to really enjoy them. There are so many lessons here that align with us asking God for what we want; I don't really know where to begin.

Perhaps the first one that comes to mind is the fact that I derived this little lesson from a child, as in *Matthew 18:3 (NIV): "unless you change and become like little children."* But the one that really hits home for me is the fact that she trusted me enough to temporarily give me possession of it once again. How many times has God waited for us to just take a step back and hand him our burden or perhaps our treasure, knowing he will transform the situation or issue into our ultimate good?

This is "knocking" or "beckoning the Holy Spirit" in its most innocent form. Sometimes we hand the bag of cookies back to him to open, and instead of opening them immediately and handing them back to us, he turns and walks toward the door. And we, somewhat like children, but in this case spoiled brats; stomp out of the room before he opens the door that reveals the steak and lobster dinner waiting on the table. Then there are some of us, myself included, that never considered giving the bag back to him in the first place, and the only thing that keeps us from biting his hand is the fact that we are too involved trying to chew the top off the bag ourselves. Or, we are too busy fighting others over the bag, to actually hand it back to him.

I learned a little something from one of my other grandchildren last summer as well, when it comes to the business of asking and seeking and the motives that lie behind it. My grandson Treyson and I were walking into the grocery store, when he asked me if we could go into the store next door. This was one of those stores that advertise the fact that everything is a dollar. We referred to them as "dime stores" when I was his age. But with the rate of inflation, everything in this store is just one dollar. He knows that I am an easy mark; usually paying off like an ATM machine once we hit the toy aisle. But this time I thought I would throw him a curve, asking him: "Well, we can go in there, but how much money do you have on you?" The question soon backfired on me in a most innocent and amazing way, when he stated: "I have a dollar, so I can get anything I want." I guess it is all in your perspective!

This one little dollar store story teaches us so many lessons when it comes to "seeking." When we relate that to the Kingdom of God, we may know that when we have the Spirit, when we truly seek the Holy Spirit, as in the One within the Spirit, we actually have "anything" that we want. *Matthew 6:33 (NIV): But seek first his kingdom and his righteousness, and all these things will be added to you as well.*

James even adds a little bit more to the liability of asking in *James 4: 1-3 (NIV): What causes fights and quarrels among you? Don't they come from your desires that battle within you? You want something but don't get it. You kill and covet but you cannot have what you want. You quarrel and fight. You do not have because you do not ask God. When you ask, you do not receive, because you ask with wrong motives, that you may spend what you get on your pleasures.* Try sincerely asking God for wisdom; answers and insight that will benefit his kingdom by making you a better steward of your own life. See what God creates not only within the kingdom, but in you as well, through the power of the Holy Spirit. He does not disappoint!

I have a third grandchild that is yet to teach me any lessons. I will give him the full benefit of the doubt however, as he is "three days" old as I write this. I am sure God will eventually give me some kind of sign when he is ready, as his name is Jonah. And for those of you who are not laughing right now; you may "seek" *Matthew 16:1-4 (NIV)*. But since you may be new to this seeking business, I will give you a free pass on this one. And by the way, just a little background before the Scripture, Jonah was in the whale for three days, just as Christ was in the tomb for three days, before both emerged to do a little prophesying. *Matthew 16: 1-4 (NIV): The Pharisees and the Sadducees came to Jesus and tested him by asking him to show them a sign from heaven. He replied, "When evening comes you say, 'It will be fair weather, for the sky is red,' and in the morning, 'Today it will be stormy, for the sky is red and overcast.' You know how to interpret the appearance of the sky, but you cannot interpret the signs of the times. A wicked and adulterous generation looks for a miraculous sign, but none will be given it except the sign of Jonah."*

PRAYER POINT:

Instruct me in the true art of prayer within the Holy Spirit, petitioning through your Word, and asking out of love for the glorification of the Father.

AISLE NINE

Moderation Flirtation

Moderation is a frequently tempting mistress. I am no longer satisfied with just one kiss.

Luke 24:5 (NIV): Why do you look for the living among the dead?

Luke 19: 41-42 (NIV): As he approached Jerusalem and saw the city, he wept over it and said, "If you, even you, had only known on this day what would give you peace – but now it is hidden from your eyes."

If you remember on Aisle Seven, I told you we would discuss moderation. So true to my word; here is the "clean up on Aisle Nine." That's correct; I am going to come clean with you. I have known several people through the years who have had a glass of wine with dinner, a taste of sparkling wine during a celebration, an ice cold beer on a summer afternoon or a single malt scotch by the fireplace on a cold winter's night and never had a problem with it. If you have not guessed already, by the endearing circumstances I placed on each one of these libations, I have been there before myself. But while I have admired them, I am certainly not one of those people. The only times I was able to have a "single" malt scotch were when the numerous glasses of scotch I was drinking were not of the blended variety, thus the term: single malt. I apologize for lingering over the scotch, but felt a little more definition may be in order for the non-drinkers.

Moderation has never been part of my genetic make-up, and this has been a reality ever since I can remember. I was always the kid that never had any Trick or Treat candy twenty-four hours after the fact. To this day, I have never really been able to figure out why they put vending machine cookie packs in re-sealable bags or why anyone would take the time to read how many servings actually come in the container, when the simple answer is usually: one or not nearly enough! Hands down however, the greatest offender has to be those pre-popped bags of pop-corn that hook you with: Only 150 calories per serving. Then, right before you throw the empty bag away after inhaling it in one sitting; you notice there were also 150 servings in the bag. You do the math!

I do not mean to make light of it, because I realize moderation or the lack thereof is a serious problem. We all face our own demons. It is important to bear in mind, while we may be in very separate battles our mutual ally is Christ, and he has given us the Holy Spirit to wage our individual wars. These wars have been going on for quite some time. And they will most certainly continue until Christ calls us home. The victory is ours if we will call upon the resources and power of the Holy Spirit: *Revelation 12: 7-9 (NIV): "And there was war in heaven. Michael and his angels fought against the dragon, and the dragon and his angels fought back. But he was not strong enough, and they lost their place in heaven. The great dragon was hurled down – that ancient serpent called the devil, or Satan, who leads the whole world astray. He was hurled to the earth, and his angels with him."*

I have the ability to take some of my dinner home in a doggy bag. Well, sometimes, even though my dog has never had the opportunity to eat so much as a crouton from one of those foam boxes. But my down-fall lies in the fact that I probably will not need to keep track of the cork once it is out of the Chardonnay. Which sooner than later (and usually sooner), leads me to *Habakkuk 2: 4-5 (NIV): "See, he is puffed up; his desires are not upright-but the righteous will live by faith-indeed, wine betrays him; he is arrogant and never at rest."*

If you do battle against the excessive grapes and your friends notice you have switched your ale from multiple choices to simply root beer, chances are you may hear one of the following Scriptures: *1 Timothy 5:23 (NIV): "Stop drinking only water, and use a little wine because of your stomach and your frequent illnesses." Matthew 11: 18-19 (NIV)* is another all time favorite from my buddies bellied up to the bar. Jesus is telling the crowd how fickle they were when it came to prophets, including John the Baptist and himself: *"For John came neither eating nor drinking, and they say, 'He has a demon.' The Son of Man came eating and drinking, and they say, 'Here is a glutton and a drunkard, a friend of tax collectors and "sinners."' But wisdom is proved right by her actions."*

OK, so Paul did recommend Timothy drink some wine now and then with his water that had no telling what kind of bacteria in it at the time, for the good of his stomach. If you will notice, he definitely utilizes the term: *"use a little wine"* in the interest of portion control. The question of moderation, when it comes to Jesus, is answered very clearly in the Scripture. Even though Christ turned water into wine; the first miracle at a wedding party in Cana, and danced with the Non-Baptists and drank wine with the tax collectors, the assurance that he never over indulged is given to us in the latter part of *Matthew 11:19 (NIV): "But wisdom is proved right by her actions."* We may rest assured that the Son of God, Jesus Christ, never grieved the Holy Spirit, as they are "One in the Father": The Holy Trinity. Moderation was always the order of the day, even though he was under the influence of excessive joy on many occasions. This is a model we would do well to duplicate.

If you are drinking to excess, you are binding the hands of the Holy Spirit and limiting his power. Ounce per ounce you are trading joy and peace for a very dangerous, temporary and deceptive pacifier. Christ tells us in *Mark 3: 27(NIV)*: *"In fact, no one can enter a strong man's house and carry off his possessions unless he first ties up the strong man. Then, he can rob his house."* Jesus was differentiating himself from Satan, as the "teachers of the law," the hypocritical Pharisee types, accused him of driving out demons because he was a demon. The underlying metaphor here is the fact that Christ was binding the hands of Satan, through his power, which was the power of the Holy Spirit. Therefore, through the process of reversing this paradigm, if we have bound the Holy Spirit's power, by replacing it with another spirit, which in this case is a spirit of excess, we are about to watch helplessly as those powers and principalities of darkness rob our house.

1 Thessalonians 5:19 (NIV): *"Do not put out the Spirit's fire; do not treat prophecies with contempt. Test everything. Hold on to the good. Avoid every kind of evil."* When you drink to excess, you extinguish the Spirit's power within you. Once this occurs, it is only a matter of time, usually a very small window, where good is replaced by evil. God will not be mocked, so ask for help in the form of the Holy Spirit. The moment you feel tempted by that second or third glass; the one that will surely quench the Spirit's fire, you should look to the Holy Spirit for your rescue. In this case, instead of putting out the Spirit's fire, you should call upon the Holy Spirit to be the fireman: "In case of emergency, break glass."

Consider where you fall on the issue of moderation, or better yet; where you don't fall. If you are one that can control it; then so be it and may God bless you. If you have a problem with it, you need to consider the greatest gift from God since salvation; which is the power of the Holy Spirit within you. You may want to order a different kind of Spirit from the ultimate bartender.

John 4:10 (NIV): *Jesus answered her, "If you knew the gift of God and who it is that asks you for a drink, you would have asked him and he would have given you living water."*

It is also very important to keep those who may be struggling with it in mind as well, no matter where their battles may be waged: *Romans 14:21(NIV): "It is better not to eat meat or drink wine or to do anything else that will cause your brother to fall."* Even if you do not have a problem with excess, your total abstinence in certain situations may be the difference in another individual's challenges. Christ tells us to look out for our neighbors in *Matthew 22: 34-40 (NIV)*, when the Pharisees try to trap him with a trick question: *Hearing that Jesus had silenced the Sadducees, the Pharisees got together. One of them, an expert in the law, tested him with this question: "Teacher, which is the greatest commandment in the Law?" Jesus replied: "'Love the Lord your God with all your heart and with all your soul and with all your mind.' This is the first and greatest commandment. And the second is like it: 'Love your neighbor as yourself.' All the Law and the Prophets hang on these two commandments."* So keep your neighbors in mind, and do whatever it takes to mind their struggles, wherever and whenever they may occur.

I dearly love those six verses in the latter part of *Matthew 22* as they outline the mistake the Pharisees and the Sadducees made; being strict religious types that vacuum all of the love and Spirit out of a so called faith, leaving one with an empty and powerless religion void of love. We have to be careful not to follow their battle tactics as we wage war on the natural spirit of man; making sure we have our priorities straight, which is to follow the Law (The Ten Commandments) by the power of the Spirit, and not pursue the Law on our own merit, expecting the Spirit to follow.

Christ gave us the Holy Spirit as the ultimate power gift and he gave it to us out of love. Paul explains in *1 Corinthians 13* that our actions, even with the best of intent, if void of love, do not matter. Christ gives us the Spirit of his love, and he gives it to us by faith and hope. Paul reminds us in *1 Corinthians 13:13 (NIV): "And now these three remain: faith, hope and love. But the greatest of these is love."* And through that love, through that sacrifice, we have the gift of the Holy Spirit, the Alpha and the Omega, and therefore should always remember: *Ephesians 4:30 (NIV): "And do not grieve the Holy Spirit of God, with whom you were sealed for the day of redemption."*

LEAVE ON SHELF:

I can revisit this in moderation, even though I have historically failed. Wrong!

ADD TO CART:

Ask for wisdom to know your limits; which may very well be zero, and order the Spirit to resist.

If you have a history of alcohol abuse the decision to take another little side trip, weekend excursion, vacation or even a holiday visit to the make believe land of moderation always ends in disaster. My last few sabbaticals from abstinence looked a little like this:

Plan A: This one occurred the Friday after Thanksgiving, which is the day we decorate our home for the Christmas season. I cannot warn you enough to be constantly aware of vacations and holidays, as sad as that may seem. I spent most of the day scaling the attic stairs, which is actually one of those pull-down ladder deathtraps. I traverse this approximately four times per year with spring cleaning in May, Halloween and Thanksgiving down in early October, then Halloween and Thanksgiving up the day after Thanksgiving, along with Christmas down the same day, and then Christmas up the day before New Year's Eve; which is another traditional bear trap if you're not paying attention.

I now have all of the Christmas decorations firmly in place with the exception of the lights, because the extension cords have vanished again this year. So totally exhausted and feeling a bit sentimental, which are another two allies of this negative holiday spirit, I decide it would not be a bad idea to just open that bottle of wine that one of my associates gave me as a Christmas gift last year. I had discovered it earlier, when I rescued Jesus and the rest of the nativity party from the back of the towel closet in the bathroom. I had honestly forgotten about it until that day. But upon my rediscovery, I thought it would be a good idea to re-gift it, rather than just letting it go bad or throwing it away.

After some twenty death-defying trips to the attic, and staring at the remains of the smoked turkey, I thought: "What the heck, why don't I just open it and split it with my wife. We could have one glass each to-night and one glass a piece tomorrow." Upon running this little picture of moderation past my wife, who was lying on the couch with what I be-lieve was either cotton Christmas snow or a chunk of attic insulation in her hair, she was an easy mark.

Needless to say, all four glasses were gone by the end of the night, with my wife downing one and yours truly exercising a little early Christmas magic by making the other three disappear.

Plan B: Waking up with just a little ping of a headache, I was able to blame it on the attic ladder, which totally dismissed any "day-after" guilt by this post Thanksgiving turkey. And as evening rolled around, I was able to justify the fact that we would just drink wine, in moderation of course, through the Holidays. I am unable to remember if this plan went out through the backdoor or the front door, or whether it just went up the chimney. But as far as moderation, it was Happy New Year to all, right up until the next Halloween.

Plan C: Beware of the change in seasons, as they casually lead to old haunts. It's Memorial Day, the beginning of summer. The birds and the bees, the sunscreen and the shorts I should have donated to char-ity some five years ago are all out! We are a traditional family, and this always involves visiting the gravesites of our loved ones. This also comes complete with nostalgic memories of my dad at the beach; with a beer in one hand, a cigarette in the other, and a big old summer smile on his face. There is something about the smell of suntan lotion which still takes me right back there to this day.

After a day of fun, sun, and graveside memories we wound up in a Mexican food restaurant. Well hold on to your sombrero, because the first thing that hits me is the couple at the table next to ours. These folks are drinking beer from those goblets the size of beach balls, rimmed in salt and lime, with frost running down the side of the glass. Not that I lingered long over it, but soon came to the decision that I could have a beer or two this summer with a meal. Well, needless to say, by Labor Day, I was able to purchase new Halloween decorations from all of the aluminum we had cashed in by the end of the summer. And I might have had enough money to buy new Thanksgiving decorations as well, had I not switched to margaritas sometime around the Fourth of July.

Once again, I do not mean to make light of a serious situation, but wanted to give you the reality of the depths of this deception. It always seems so easy and natural to conform to my old traditions, without the power of the Holy Spirit. *Romans 12:2 (NIV): Do not conform any longer to the pattern of this world, but be transformed by the renewing of your mind. Then you will be able to test and approve what God's will is – his good, pleasing and perfect will.* I am printing three copies of *Romans 12:2*: One for my swim suits, one for my Halloween decorations box and one for the top of the Christmas tree. Through the power of the Holy Spirit, and only through that power, will I be able to refrain from becoming "all wet," keep from being "tricked" as I justify the fact I can "treat myself," and last but certainly not least, see this Word of God as the light, the Star, which leads us to the Savior's birth: A Merry Christmas to all, and to all a good night!

PRAYER POINT:

Teach me through the wisdom and power of the Holy Spirit to define my individual points of moderation and excess within each specific area of my life.

AISLE TEN

Stumbling

I want to get this right, to arrive at a place called contentment, with no desire to revisit iniquities.

Isaiah 61:1 (NIV): The Spirit of the Sovereign Lord is on me, because the Lord has anointed me to preach good news to the poor. He has sent me to bind up the broken hearted, to proclaim freedom for the captives and release from darkness for the prisoners.

❦

One has to remember that the road to becoming more like Christ is a work in progress. The process will surely involve setbacks and defeats. Saint Peter, who assured Jesus he would die with him if it came right down to it, managed to deny Christ three times between the Last Supper and the time the rooster crowed before breakfast the very next day: *Matthew 26: 31-75 (NIV)*. But to give Peter a pass, that was before the Holy Spirit was made available to all of us, even if Peter was standing in front of the "Real Physical Deal" at the time he pledged his undying allegiance. Can you imagine what Peter must have felt like when the fine feathered alarm clock reminded him of his inadequacy the night before, realizing what he had temporarily forfeited for lack of courage and faith? Here again, Peter was making promises from his own position of strength or lack thereof. So when it came down to an undying allegiance without the power of the Holy Spirit, it was Peter's allegiance that was actually the only part of Peter that did die that night. I can imagine Peter's remorse, because I have been there; failing to pray, step back, and re-engage the power of the Holy Spirit, trading it all in for a false and temporary comfort. Discouragement, like Peter experienced that night, not only makes cowards of us all, but without the power of the Holy Spirit, will soon turn our dreams into nightmares.

Joel 1:5 (NIV): "Wake up all you drunkards, and weep! Wail, all you drinkers of wine; wail because of the new wine, for it has been snatched from your lips." What a night! The *"new wine,"* in this instance, is the abundant life you have in Christ through the power of the Holy Spirit. Yes, beware of the night my friend, but for those of you who face these demons during the daylight hours, the Holy Spirit is on call twenty-four-seven. This should serve as a reminder that you don't have to be a chicken in between the times the rooster crows.

I am convinced that the Holy Bible often utilizes the term "night or nighttime" as a metaphor for darkness, meaning darkness as opposed to light, or good versus evil. Remember, in the beginning, as in the beginning of the earth, which takes place in *Genesis 1: 3-4 (NIV): And God said, "Let there be light," and there was light. God saw that the light was good and he separated the light from the darkness.* This was the beginning of the separation of light and darkness, which is a metaphor that runs all the way through the Bible. Jesus Christ explains that he is in fact the light of the world in *John 8: 12 (NIV): When Jesus spoke again to the people, he said, "I am the light of the world. Whoever follows me will never walk in darkness, but will have the light of life."* Christ even proclaims that his followers are *the light of the world: Matthew 5: 14 (NIV) You are the light of the world. A city on a hill cannot be hidden.* This leads me to believe that any time we circumvent the Holy Spirit by giving way to the power of man's natural spirit; we are actually short circuiting the light of Christ and giving the darkness of sin a free reign within our lives. God also orders a *"darkness that can be felt"* to fall on the Egyptians in *Exodus 10: 21-23 (NIV): Then the Lord said to Moses, "Stretch out your hand toward the sky so that darkness will spread over Egypt –darkness that can be felt." So Moses stretched out his hand toward the sky, and total darkness covered all Egypt for three days. No one could see anyone else or leave his place for three days. Yet all the Israelites had light in the places where they lived.*

If you have ever fought an addiction like excessive drinking first hand, you are well aware that the urges and the temptations do not necessarily wait for the sun to go down. If you are inclined to drink to excess, there is no hard and fast rule that you will necessarily wait until "happy hour," which is probably why they coined the phrase: "It's five-o'clock somewhere." But in the case of light versus darkness, perhaps the term: "It's dark somewhere," would be more appropriate. Therefore, I have always been fond of *Psalm 91: 5-6 (NIV): You will not fear the terror of night, nor the arrow that flies by day, nor the pestilence that stalks the darkness, nor the plague that destroys at midday.* It offers us a twenty-four hour insurance policy from the Holy Spirit. This Scripture worked particularly well for me when I was quitting cigarettes, picturing *"the arrow that flies by day"* as the cigarettes and the illnesses they cause as the *"plague that destroys at midday."* So when the Bible mentions nighttime, keep in mind this may also be a reference to darkness, like we are about to see in *1 Thessalonians.*

1 Thessalonians 4: 7-8 (NIV): "For those who sleep, sleep at night, and those who get drunk, get drunk at night. But since we belong to the day, let us be self-controlled, putting on faith and love as a breastplate, and the hope of salvation as a helmet." Did you catch the *"faith and love"* part, as well as the *"hope of salvation"* in *1 Thessalonians?* Paul is telling us that we have to be prepared for these challenges, and the Holy Spirit will equip us with faith and love to cover our hearts, as well as the hope of our salvation or the vision of what we can become in Christ; our true and complete selves.

I want to make it perfectly clear however, that in this instance Paul is not talking about your eternal salvation being at risk. Nobody is saying that if you drink too much you are going to spend eternity in a fire pit. The hope of salvation in this instance does not mean your eternal home in heaven is at stake if you happen to stumble over the "all you can eat buffet" or have "one too many." But you are temporarily forfeiting the "abundance of salvation" or the abundant life that God promises us all this side of heaven. You were saved, and saved eternally, the moment you believed in Jesus Christ as the Son of God, sent from heaven to die for your sins. And Christ puts our minds at ease in *John 6: 38-40 (NIV): "For I have come down from heaven not to do my will but to do the will of him who sent me. And this is the will of him who sent me; that I shall not lose one of all that he has given me, but raise them up on the last day. For my Father's will is that everyone who looks to the Son and believes in him shall have eternal life, and I will raise him up at the last day." "That I shall not lose one of all that he has given me,"* is actually you in this case; the moment you believed and accepted Jesus Christ as your personal savior.

Christ even tells us in *Mark 3: 28-29 (NIV)*, after he explains that we have the ability to defeat evil spirits by the power of the Holy Spirit, that all sins will be forgiven with the exception of one, which is blasphemy against the Holy Spirit. Christ was defining *"blasphemies against the Holy Spirit"* as being an unbeliever. Christ was speaking to the Pharisees, and the short translation was the fact that they failed to believe he was the Son of God, sent to earth to die for the forgiveness of man's sin, and were therefore committing blasphemy against the very Spirit within him, which is the Holy Spirit.

So before you start believing you may have missed heaven by a few martinis or a third helping of those mashed potatoes, I have a little insurance clause that I created for just such occasions: "Hope gives wings to the imagination, and faith lends the power to fly." In other words, the Holy Spirit will furnish us with hope and power, but we have to ask for it and receive it in faith. We also need to understand that this is a continual process, and that is the reason why "faith is on loan." "Faith lends the power to fly," because faith, for the natural sinful nature of man, is not always in adequate supply. One would do well to bear this in mind. Whenever we are faced with temptation, we need to be aware of the fact that we cannot "imagine" what God has in store for us on this side of heaven. The stipulation rests in the remembrance of calling on the Holy Spirit for the power of faith, which enables us to fly. This is our hope of salvation. This is our abundant life, the role we were meant to play this side of heaven. This is the joy of our salvation on the road to our eternal salvation in heaven.

Our eternal salvation was guaranteed, once and for all, the moment we accepted Jesus Christ as our Savior. This salvation does not make us perfect however, due to our human nature. We need to understand that there will certainly be setbacks along the way. The Psalmist reassures us in *Psalm 37:23-25 (NIV): "If the Lord delights in a man's way, he makes his steps firm; though he stumble, he will not fall, for the Lord upholds him with his hand. I was young and now I am old, yet I have never seen the righteous forsaken or their children begging bread." "Though he stumble,"* in this instance, means that none of us will emerge from this Christian life without a few setbacks. But rest assured God's infinite forgiveness through the sacrifice of his Son for your sins, will always provide you with an eternal safety net.

But before you board that party bus, let me point out the shots that Paul takes as he offers a "one-two" punch in *Romans 6: 1-2 (NIV): "What shall we say, then? Shall we go on sinning so that grace may increase? By no means! We died to sin; how can we live in it any longer?"* Paul continues to seal the deal for us in *Romans 8: 1-2 (NIV): "Therefore, there is now no condemnation for those who are in Christ Jesus, because through Christ Jesus the law of the Spirit of life set me free from the law of sin and death."*

The next time you are tempted to order a double, whether that be a double shot or just a double order of those huge portions that are enough to feed a third-world family for two days, remember what Elisha asked of Elijah in *2 Kings 2:9 (NIV): When they had crossed, Elijah said to Elisha, "Tell me what I can do for you before I am taken from you?" "Let me inherit a double portion of your spirit," Elisha replied.* This was quite a compliment, if you consider that earlier in Elijah's ministry: *1 Kings 19:12(NIV);* Elijah was feeling a little sorry for himself due to his persecution as a prophet of the Lord. The Lord chose to strengthen Elijah's faith by coming to him in a *"gentle whisper"*. Or, as the King James Bible states it: *1 Kings 19:12 (KJV): "a still small voice".* Either version delivers the point, which is to wait upon the *"gentle whisper"* or *"the still small voice"* of the Holy Spirit, whenever we may begin to stumble a bit. Nonbelievers just refer to this as their conscience, but seem to have a limited amount of success when faced with acts of the sinful nature. So letting your "conscience be your guide" often ends in the blind leading the blind. *Luke 6:39 (NIV): He also told them this parable: Can a blind man lead a blind man? Will they not both fall into a pit?* The human nature is so corrupt that the heart of flesh can often undermine the conscience. *Jeremiah 17:9 (NIV): "The heart is deceitful above all things and beyond cure. Who can understand it?"*

Yes, order a double! That is, a double portion of the Holy Spirit:

Galatians 5:5 (NIV) "But by faith we eagerly await through the Spirit the righteousness for which we hope." The *"righteousness for which we hope,"* is exclusively within the power of the Holy Spirit. The righteousness which Paul speaks of in Galatians 5 encompasses the guarantee of eternal life as well as abundant life within the here and now, if we will only stay within the Spirit.

Psalm 104:30 (NIV) "When you send your Spirit, they are created, and you renew the face of the earth." Through the power of the Holy Spirit we are newly created and receive the full realization of our true being in Christ. This power enables us to truly become the individuals we were created to be.

Please know, that stumbling will occur; and though perfection will never be achieved this side of heaven, we will continue to improve and rest in the peace of knowing we have grace and mercy from Christ, while we grow in the increasing power of the Spirit.

Lamentations 3: 22-24 (NIV): Because of the Lord's great love we are not consumed, for his compassions never fail. They are new every morning; great is your faithfulness. I say to myself, "The Lord is my portion; therefore I will wait for him."

As for Peter, the one who denied him three times in the same night, he made an incredible comeback, once he received the Holy Spirit: *1 Peter 3:18 (NIV): "For Christ died for sins once for all, the righteous for the unrighteous, to bring you to God. He was put to death in the body but made alive by the Spirit."* Hopefully, you caught the part about Christ dying for sins *"once for all,"* which certainly means he died for your sins that you have committed as well as the multitude of sins you will commit. The really good news is that I am talking about the sins you will commit within the course of tomorrow, the sins from yesterday, and yes, also today! Keeping that in mind, stay the course, just as Paul asks for us in *Ephesians 1:17 (NIV)*, letting us know this is a growth process: *"I keep asking that the God of our Lord Jesus Christ, the glorious Father, may give you the Spirit of wisdom and revelation, so that you may know him better."*

LEAVE ON SHELF:

Dismiss the shame of believing that the Lord may very well have a limit on the gift of the Holy Spirit when it comes to your repeated failures.

ADD TO CART:

Know that stumbling will occur, but it is a growth process, as long as we "get to our feet" again, through the grace of our Lord Jesus Christ and the power of the Holy Spirit.

I may have the ultimate "stumbling story" or at least I would put this one up against a lot of contenders. I attempted to enter the ministry as a college student. The emphasis is on "attempted," but it actually had nothing to do with my young age. My failure was due to the fact that I was driven exclusively by my own willpower; void of any assistance or aid from the Holy Spirit's power. I made the decision to become a minister even though I was not sure how to define the position at that particular point in my life. The word "position" actually gives you a big hint here as to my misguided personal endeavor. Not that my intentions were anything but genuine, as I was no doubt a Christian. But I believe it was the thumbnail sketch of the "occupation" that I dedicated my life to that day, which led me astray. I do not recall if my "position" included a private evangelical jet, but I am quite sure it did involve a pulpit that was illuminated by several spotlights in a very crowded arena; if you get my drift. A very wise friend of mine, who eventually became a minster as a full time occupational position, even told me that the "license" I would receive could be a very dangerous piece of paper, if not kept in a proper perspective. I now know that perspective must rest within the power of the Holy Spirit.

When my entourage left the temple that day, being led by their recently licensed Pharisee, we wound up at a certain cafeteria, where we proceeded to celebrate my newly acquired position. The cafeteria went out of business two years later and became the new site of a big disco; which is a nightclub, for those of you that are too young to remember Saturday Night Fever. For those of you who may not believe that God works with a certain degree of irony when dealing with misplaced motives; a very disillusioned recent college graduate worked there as a bartender and then the manager. Yes, it was yours truly, and it was a "license" to a lifestyle of several years of severe stumbling. I was stumbling and bumbling, which is actually a term I assign to rebellion with excess. Stumbling and bumbling until the One who created me, once again, made me aware of the ultimate "occupation," which is the power of his Spirit within me: *Isaiah 46:4 (NIV): "Even to your old age and gray hairs I am he, I am he who will sustain you. I have made you and I will carry you; I will sustain you and I will rescue you."*

PRAYER POINT:

Remind me of your abundant forgiveness; strengthen me within the Spirit as I face current and future challenges.

AISLE ELEVEN

Bad Company

Fair weather friends share troubles and false solutions, while staring into the glass, avoiding eye contact at all cost; the bloodshot windows of the soul.

Proverbs 18:24 (NIV): A man of many companions may come to ruin but there is a friend who sticks closer than a brother.

*T*est the spirits, that is, before you reach for one. Examine their origin and put them to the 100% proof test, as *1 John 4: 1-3 (NIV)* explains: *"Dear friends, do not believe every spirit, but test the spirits to see whether they are from God, because many false prophets have gone out into the world. This is how you recognize the Spirit of God: Every spirit that acknowledges that Jesus Christ has come in the flesh is from God, but every spirit that does not acknowledge Jesus is not from God. This is the spirit of the antichrist, which you have heard is coming and even now is already in the world."*

False prophets and corrupt spirits have one thing in common, which is the innate ability to isolate you from the Holy Spirit, substituting a slightly altered lifestyle which eventually leaves you in a fearful solitude. Yes, even in a packed bar, one may find they are "lonely in a crowd," because they are mingling with alien spirits. Granted, these may be "natural spirits" and at times even appear to be "kindred spirits," but they are not from where you truly belong; the residence of overriding peace, generating from an everlasting joy. So the chances of God enabling you to find long term peace and companionship there are pretty much obsolete. Remember, God cannot be mocked, and therefore even the slightest compromise can leave you marooned on the rocks.

Chances are; what is floating on those rocks or under that lime wedge is adding to your fear rather than dissolving it. Yes, the simple fact of the matter is, not only do you have the wrong spirit in your hand, but you very well may be sitting next to a few false prophets. And it is only a matter of time before you find yourself "all wet." In this instance, "all wet" is the direct opposite of "dry." But I have always detested that term, due to the fact that abstinence from excess, while living in the Spirit, or being filled with the Holy Spirit rather than excessive spirits, leaves you anything but "dry." On the other hand however, I have seen a number of folks who attempt this on their own accord, which is where we derive the term: dry drunk.

Now, before you start thinking I am casting all of your old drinking buddies with horns and pitchforks in their hands, as well as condemning the "evils of the demon rum," let me remind you that I was the one that gave you the moderation pass back on Aisle Nine. Of course this is all contingent on the fact that you and your friends live within the boundaries of that moderation. My old friends that own clubs and restaurants will probably hate me for saying this, but if you find yourself plodding through the day to get to your favorite watering hole, where moderation soon melts away, you may find yourself with the wrong menu in your hand. *1 Corinthians 15: 32-34 (NIV): "If I fought wild beasts in Ephesus for merely human reasons, what have I gained? If the dead are not raised, 'Let us eat and drink, for tomorrow we die.' Do not be misled: 'Bad company corrupts good character.' Come back to your senses and quit sinning, for there are some who are ignorant of God—I say this to your shame."*

You don't even have to be your own judge when it comes to such matters. Turn it over to the Holy Spirit in prayer and let him be your guide. After all, you could be dining and drinking with saints, but here are three parameters you may want to tuck under the cocktail napkin:

Isaiah 5: 11-12 (NIV): Woe to those who rise early in the morning to run after their drinks, who stay up late at night till they are inflamed with wine. They have harps and lyres at their banquets, tambourines and flutes and wine, but they have no regard for the deeds of the Lord, no respect for the work of his hands. This can start with something as innocent as a few beers before a late morning college football game and manifest itself twenty years later in a 38 year old man waking up and remembering the cabinet is empty and he still has an hour before the liquor stores open.

Isaiah 5: 22-23 (NIV): Woe to those who are heroes at drinking wine and champions at mixing drinks, who acquit the guilty for a bribe, but deny justice to the innocent. And you were probably thinking that beer-bongs, gelatin shots, and boilermakers were a new thing.

1 Corinthians 5:11 (NIV): But now I am writing you that you must not associate with anyone who calls himself a brother but is sexually immoral or greedy, an idolater or a slanderer, a drunkard or a swindler. With such a man do not even eat. You wouldn't walk up on a pack of dingoes while they were dining over a kill, so why dine with wolves in lambs clothing. I hate to visit gambling once again, but as the old saying goes: "If you sit down at a poker table and don't see a sucker, get up, because you're it!" I know it probably seems like I have had a problem with gambling, as much as I gravitate back to it. However, I can assure you this was never one of my vices. Not that I am bragging, because I think I have all of the other ones covered.

Admittedly, I may have been a little rough with that last comparison, meaning the wild dogs and all. Granted, sexual immorality, greed, slander and swindling can be found most anywhere these days, as *1 Timothy 4:1 (NIV)* tells us: *"The Spirit clearly says that in later times some will abandon the faith and follow deceiving spirits and things taught by demons."* But, if you are entirely honest with yourself, you have to admit there is a greater chance of "heartburn" where spirits of "firewater" are consumed as the main venue.

By now you are probably thinking to yourself what a tall order this is really going to be, after all, you have associated with this group for most of your life now. But take heart or better yet the Holy Spirit. Because if they are the real deal as far as true friendship goes, they may go for a season without you, but eventually they will honor you for your choices and you will maintain these friendships throughout your lifetime. Your genuine friends will stand this fire test, but some will show their true colors, and it is better for you that you know this now: *Nahum 1:10 (NIV): "They will be entangled among the thorns and drunk from their wine; they will be consumed like dry stubble."*

I know this is scary stuff at first, and sometimes terrifyingly lonely, but you have to remember, you are never alone. *1 Corinthians 4:14 (NIV): "If you are insulted because of the name of Christ, you are blessed, for the Spirit of glory and of God rests on you."* Yes, there are better things to come. You will be surprised, once you step out in faith and prayer while asking for the power of the Holy Spirit to sustain you, how soon they will arrive. Leave the fear on the rocks or perhaps just sitting at the high top table, and take these words from Paul to his true friend Timothy as your new marching orders:

2 *Timothy 1:7 (NIV): "For God did not give us a spirit of timidity* (KJV: fear), *but a spirit of power, of love and of self-discipline."* It is interesting to note that we are not only given the courage to

resist temptations, as in the spirit of self-discipline, but also the spirit of power, which tells us we are given the energy to form new relationships and new opportunities, as we proceed within the wisdom of the Holy Spirit. Plus, you get an added bonus, with both of these qualities wrapped within the love of Christ. We now know we have been given this Spirit out of love, so we may pioneer new worlds with that same love, accompanied by power and self-discipline.

2 Timothy 1: 11-14 (NIV): "And of this gospel I was appointed a herald and an apostle and a teacher. That is why I am suffering as I am. Yet I am not ashamed, because I know whom I have believed, and am convinced that he is able to guard what I have entrusted to him for that day. What you heard from me, keep as the pattern of sound teaching, with faith and love in Christ Jesus. Guard the good deposit that was entrusted to you—guard it with the help of the Holy Spirit who lives in us." The Holy Spirit enables me to transition through this very temporary state of conflict, constantly giving me the vision of hope, as we transform the imagination of dreams into a joy filled reality.

I want to leave you with one last word of advice here in regard to your old buddies. Don't expect to find that perfect friend, because nobody is perfect, including you! We are all born into the world with this human nature, so looking for the perfect friend is like looking for the perfect church, which is not going to happen either. But do not despair, because the One who paid for your salvation, and gave you the power in the Spirit, also stands ready to be that perfect friend, while at the same time, making your body the perfect church: the home for the Holy Spirit, whether you are hungry or thirsty. *John 6: 35(NIV): Then Jesus declared, "I am the bread of life. He who comes to me will never go hungry, and he who believes in me will never be thirsty."* I also have another piece of good news for you on the friendship front. You will not remain a one hit wonder for long, meaning Christ as your only friend. Once you get your heart right through the power of the Holy Spirit, aligning your heart's desires with God's will, you will not long for kindred spirits. Of course, I am speaking of the human variety and not just something floating around the club circuit.

LEAVE ON SHELF:

Some of your old acquaintances: both liquid and human, need to be dismissed permanently or suspended at least for a season.

ADD TO CART:

Your new vision should rest in the fact that the Holy Spirit will comfort and guide you as you make what may first appear to be awkward decisions. You should pray for the wisdom to discern spirits, separating the Spirit of God from the spirit of the antichrist. Continue to pray for the ones you need to leave behind for now, loving them in the true Spirit.

Sometimes the business of discerning spirits can be a little tricky. Therefore, you always want to make sure that you are being led by the Holy Spirit, instead of vice-versa, with the emphasis on "vice." My case in point would be the time I last saw my great-aunt in the nursing home where she lived shortly after a succession of strokes. She was my great-aunt with emphasis on great, as far as being one of my spiritual heroes and icons from the earliest time I could remember. And the memories all came flooding back that day: reading Bible stories, rocking me to sleep, preparing lunches and dinners, sleepovers in her duplex upstairs from where we lived below, Saturday morning cartoons together; providing I could ascend those creaky old wooden stairs at that early morning hour, without waking my dad and being ordered back to bed. And then, of course, the infinite games of Candy Land, which I always won, believe it or not.

"If we were home, I would fix you something for dinner." These were the last words she would ever say to me, as she passed away two weeks later. And in that two week period, I never could muster the courage to visit again. Between my tears and the damage of her strokes I just could not endure what I had perceived God had allowed.

Well, to say I had my spirits a little crossed up that day was definitely an understatement. I actually remember thinking that if he treats his people like this, why not "*eat, drink, and be merry*" as Paul states in *1 Corinthians 15:32 (NIV)*. I mean, after all, I know that I am saved by faith, so why not enjoy this ride a little bit more, since this is what can obviously happen to a near perfect saint.

Hopefully, by now, you have seen the error of my ways, as a sixteen year old kid that obviously knew it all. But it wasn't until several years later, when the Holy Spirit led me to the realization that the spirit I carried out of the nursing home, the one that told me it was God's fault, was actually the spirit of the antichrist. That's correct; this is the same spirit that often tells us that the results of obedience are not always guaranteed. This is the same spirit that may just whisper in your ear, that you can have your cake and eat it too, because after all, the results are basically the same for everyone in the long run. And this is the same spirit that told Eve if she ate the forbidden fruit, she wouldn't really die, but conveniently left out the part that she would surely wish she were dead.

Yes, I had my spirits crossed that day, but have since realized that the Spirit of Truth, the one that enabled my great-aunt to live a full and abundant life, is the same Spirit that will reunite us. A different old wooden structure; the Cross of Calvary, will enable that dinner party to take place again someday. Long gone will be the old creaky wooden stairs that sometimes prevented this fellowship.

So I must continue to pull the cards, and someday my passage will be as easy as landing on the lollipop square, which always permitted you to advance without effort, so far ahead of your admiring opponent, who would always make sure you were the first to arrive at the gingerbread house in Candy Land.

"If we were home, I would fix you something for dinner." This is my childhood memory and my eternal hope within the Holy Spirit. Perhaps she is at the stove of the gingerbread house, waiting for the One who makes this reunion possible to jubilantly invite me home for dinner: *Revelation 21: 3-7 (NIV): And I heard a loud voice from the throne saying, "Now the dwelling of God is with men, and he will live with them. They will be his people, and God himself will be with them and be their God. He will wipe every tear from their eyes. There will be no more death or mourning or crying or pain, for the old order of things has passed away."*

PRAYER POINT:

Reassure me of new beginnings within the power of the Holy Spirit.

AISLE TWELVE

Looking Back

If I would have only known then what I know now, is overshadowed by knowing this day, everything I will need to know for the future.

Psalm 110:1-3 (NIV): The Lord says to my Lord: "Sit at my right hand until I make your enemies a footstool for your feet." The Lord will extend your mighty scepter from Zion; you will rule in the midst of your enemies. Your troops will be willing on your day of battle. Arrayed in holy majesty, from the womb of the dawn you will receive the dew of your youth.

1 Peter 4:3 (NIV): "For you have spent enough time in the past doing what pagans choose to do—living in debauchery, lust, drunkenness, orgies, carousing and detestable idolatry. They think it strange that you do not plunge with them into the same flood of dissipation, and they heap abuse on you."

I thought I would start with that one, just in case you have already waded into my advice in regard to bad company on Aisle Eleven and your friends have been inquiring as to your absence or abstinence, as the case may be. So please pardon me for glancing back, but the fact of the matter is there will be many occasions to do just that. We have this little thing called the "natural spirit" or "human nature" embedded deep in our hearts, which we can all thank Adam and Eve for; if you're still looking to place the blame on something or someone else. Blaming someone else is often a characteristic of the overindulgent landscape, but since they are not here to defend themselves, I thought we may as well take a huge look back, and pin it on those two.

Speaking of looking back, Jesus Christ has some advice for us on the subject of head twisting in *Luke 9:62 (NIV): Jesus replied, "No one who puts his hand to the plow and looks back is fit for service in the kingdom of God."* While you may not picture yourself as a missionary, preacher, or ever even being associated with any type of farm instrument, the take away we have from this needs to be the fact that Christ is speaking first and foremost to the *"service in the kingdom of God"* as a service to our selves as Christians. The first service we need to perform after accepting the gift of salvation from God through the sacrifice of his Son Jesus Christ for our sins is the ultimate "labor of love," which is "plowing" into the further definition and acceptance of his Spirit within us. Pardon me for taking you back to the farm, but to turn your head on this first service is doing yourself the ultimate disservice. The Disciple Peter even utilizes the farm metaphor in *2 Peter 2:20,22 (NIV): "If they have escaped the corruption of the world by knowing our Lord Jesus Christ and are again entangled in it and overcome, they are worse off at the end than they were at the beginning. Of them the proverbs are true: 'A dog returns to its vomit,' and, 'A sow that is washed goes back to her wallowing in the mud.'"*

Take heart and remember you do not have to confront this on your own. I guess the really good news is the fact that your crops will all fail if you do try this exclusively on your own accord. So why bother, that is, without first asking for the power of the Holy Spirit. *Romans 8: 11 (NIV): "And if the Spirit of him who raised Jesus from the dead is living in you, he who raised Christ from the dead will also give life to our mortal bodies through his Spirit, who lives in you."* Not only is your eternal salvation not at stake here, because you are a child of God through the redemption and righteousness given to you by Jesus Christ, but you have the very Spirit in you that enables you to live the abundant life while you are still down here on the farm.

I am constantly intrigued by my own "gazing into the past." It always seems so enticing when watching television or a movie and you see the couple sipping Merlot from red wine glasses that are as big as your head. It always seems to be so glamorous and romantic. And I would be totally remiss, if I did not mention those beer commercials. Everyone in the beer commercials is not only forever young and energetic, but certainly having more fun than any one should possibly be allowed to have. All of this is usually taking place in the midst of a tailgate party, with enough cholesterol on the grill to kill half of Texas and not one beer gut to be found. While I realize that some people can do this in moderation, I guess I am still amazed whenever I see a movie where someone leaves a restaurant with wine still in the glass or heaven forbid, still in the bottle, which I have never experienced in real life. Couple this type of media, with the fact that we are currently living in a society where we idolize food through restaurant commercials; twenty-four-seven, and you literally have a recipe for disaster when it comes to excessive eating or drinking. I thought I could get out of this one without mentioning this, but shut my mouth, I cannot help myself. Is anyone else amazed with the concept of the borderline anorexic super models wolfing down the triple portion meals in the fast food ads?

My all time favorite, with all levity aside, is the personal one. That's right; the one that gets to me more than any of these is my own personal nemesis, which really reminds me that we are not on a level playing field. Mine is the "little voice" inside my head on Saturday afternoons that reminds me the liquor stores / wine shops are closed on Sundays in Oklahoma, even though I have had no intention of drinking on Sundays or any other day for quite some time. And you can bet, unless you have an issue with gambling, that this "little voice" is not the same "still small voice" or "gentle whisper" of the Holy Spirit, but someone or something that is definitely playing for the other team. However, I may rest assured that the power within my heart; The Holy Spirit, will overcome, if I just give him the chance to intervene on my behalf.

Just in case you were not convinced that the powers of darkness prey on your specific weaknesses, I have one more for you that is breaking news. The latest occurrence, which I just realized yesterday as I made my way into the copy center to print a proof copy of this book for the fifteenth time, is the fact that there is a liquor store or spirit shop right next door. On the marquee they advertise a monthly special which just so happens to be my all time favorite Chardonnay and Pinot Noir. These are advertised as a white and a red wine special of the month. Yes, now what are the odds of my favorite red and white featured, with prices so low it would make you blue in the face. Of course, with all of this red, white and blue, you could lose your freedom before the Fourth of July if you happen in the wrong door! I am counting on the Holy Spirit to give me "direction" and power, which is guaranteed to happen, but this did make me laugh.

When faced with the temptation of looking back; laugh in the face of it. Now, before you think I have lost my mind, let me explain. I remember the times I quit smoking, and the emphasis is on the plural, because I quit several times before incorporating the power of the Holy Spirit. The day that stands out, was the day I took my first deep breath; that is without coughing or wheezing. It was at that very moment, the Holy Spirit gave me the vision of hope, which was the fact that I could actually do this within his power. Every deep breath I took was a reminder of breathing in the power of the Holy Spirit. So what does that have to do with laughing? Well, a similar thing happened when I put down the grape juice. However, instead of a deep breath, I laughed for the first time in years. I am not talking about a courtesy laugh, like you give at the office when somebody tells a joke that is not that funny, but genuine laughter. This is the kind of laughter, where tears come out of the eyes. It was at that very moment that it dawned on me, or perhaps the Holy Spirit brought it to my attention. I had my spirit back! This was the Holy Spirit, and it was accompanied by the spirit of laughter, driven by a resounding joy and peace. Or one could say, "I haven't laughed like that since I was a child." So when tempted to gaze into the past and wallow in the melancholy, I may now laugh at the thought that drinking to excess could actually make one happy, when it is that very act that is robbing you of your happiness. That moment of truth was truly my Happy Hour, and I hope that made you laugh.

I know everyone's situation is a little different, and we all have a tendency to occasionally think that we were not given the same advantages, talents, and ability as the other guy. So naturally we are owed a bit more concession. After all, we deserve a little liquid break, given our specific circumstances. Or, if you are trying to beat this by turning to a strict conventional church life, there is a tendency to wade into this thing we call religion, for lack of a thousand better terms, and become bogged down in the formality and often pious nature of the law. This is often accompanied by the strong desire to run as fast as we can back to our creature comforts, or perhaps just distancing ourselves from these people who seem to be so far up this religious ladder that you can rarely hear them laugh or see them smile.

The important thing to remember when you find yourself in one of these "special circumstances" that "nobody else has ever faced" are the words from Paul in *1 Corinthians 10:13 (NIV): "No temptation has seized you except what is common to man. And God is faithful; he will not let you be tempted beyond what you can bear. But when you are tempted, he will also provide a way out so that you can stand up under it."* In other words: "Get over it," or better yet, look for your salvation from the Holy Spirit. God knows what you are up against. And not to minimize it, but he has been there before, with many others before you. And to this end, he will not give you more than you can take, that is, if you are confronting it through the power of the Holy Spirit. The mistake that so many of us make when interpreting *1 Corinthians 10:13: "he will also provide a way out,"* is the fact that we do not realize the power of the Holy Spirit within us is the exclusive path to conquering temptation. The power of the Holy Spirit is not only the *"way out"* that God always provides, but it is always the only *"way out!"*

If you remember on Aisle One or in *Matthew 18,* Christ tells us that we must become like children to enter the kingdom of heaven; so I like to think of revisiting the play ground we had at my grade school. Everything looked so big when you were about two feet tall. We had a great jungle gym with a huge ladder and then a giant slide on the end of it. I remember this when faced with a challenge and compare it to God's offering through the Holy Spirit. The ladder was a tough climb, and they probably do not even put anything like that on play grounds today. It was almost insurmountable by my own strength, so I had to stop and rest about every three rungs. I like to think of this as waiting on the Holy Spirit to energize you. But once you reached the top, you had to contend with the older kids. Their main objective was usually trying to force you back down the ladder. This left you with one escape route, which was the tough task of trying to get to the giant slide. The slide, in this case, is not an escape clause like the one floating in the glass, but a vehicle to the true joy experienced from life in the Spirit. As we peacefully glide back down to "becoming like a child," we therefore experience the peace and genuine joy that God offers each and every one of his children. And I can assure you the warmth found at the bottom of this "slide" eclipses the cold hollow clinking sound of the ice, as you hit the bottom of that glass.

So please remember when tempted to take one of these little trips back to that warm, fuzzy and false place you begged God to take you out of, that help is not only on the way, it is already within you. Once again there is a catch, which is the fact that you do have to ask or specifically acknowledge through prayer that the Spirit of God is within you. The Disciple John tells us in *1 John 4: 4-6 (NIV)*, that the Holy Spirit is greater than anything you may be up against: *"You, dear children, are from God and have overcome them, because the one who is in you is greater than the one who is in the world. They are from the world and therefore speak from the viewpoint of the world, and the world listens to them. We are from God, and whoever knows God listens to us; but whoever is not from God does not listen to us. This is how we recognize the Spirit of truth and the spirit of falsehood."*

Christ puts it like this, in the Gospel of John; *John 16: 13-14 (NIV)*: *"But when he, the Spirit of truth, comes, he will guide you into all truth. He will not speak on his own; he will speak only what he hears, and he will tell you what is yet to come. He will bring glory to me by taking from what is mine and making it known to you."* That, my friend, is the best Spirit you will ever put in your mouth, your mind and your heart, any time your eyes are tempted to wander. Words from the ultimate Preacher, in regard to the ultimate Spirit, are for you, wherever you may find yourself on your journey: *"He came and preached peace to you who were far away and peace to those of you who were near. For through him we both have access to the Father by one Spirit."* *Ephesians 2: 17-18 (NIV)*

LEAVE ON SHELF:

I may not be able to do this, so I better return to where I belong, before I really embarrass myself and shame God in the process. This is discouragement at its best and it is generating from the wrong spirit, to say the least.

ADD TO CART:

There will be times you are tempted to look back, so realizing this, acknowledge the power of the Holy Spirit within you, and ask for his strength which exclusively enables you to move forward.

When faced with the temptation to look back, give into that temptation. And now that you have picked yourself up from the floor, let me explain. When I say to give into it, I mean to look back, but in this case look back on the positive moments of your life. These will certainly gravitate to the times you were not misusing or abusing. Some of us have these memories with friends or family members, and some who have walked within the Spirit of God in the past, will be able to remember his wondrous love and the joy which was made complete within his Spirit.

Then there are some of us who are lucky enough to have had both. But before you start feeling sorry for yourself, I would ask you to pray about this within the Holy Spirit, and he will certainly bring someone or someplace to mind, who accompanies a joy filled memory. Thank God for the power of the Holy Spirit in not only remembering that person or place from your past, but thank him out of faith, that he will certainly create similar circumstances and relationships going forward.

For the time being however, I do not want to steal the thunder from the future, which in this case is on the very next Aisle. And for those of you who are gloating over having both opportunities to look back, I would leave you with this: *Luke 12:48 (NIV): From everyone who has been given much, much will be demanded; and from the one who has been entrusted with much, much more will be asked.*

And now, please afford me the opportunity to share with you one of my all time favorite opportunities to look back, which believe it or not, actually involves the time when I was a child. If you have not guessed it by now, at the risk of sounding like a momma's boy, it was and still is my mom.

She was so many different entities to me; a great mom, a friend, a teacher, sometimes a father, and as early as my memory may journey back through those childhood days; a fellow pirate on the ships we sailed together with the plum tree as the mast, and a very admirable enemy General, who valiantly led the opposing toy soldier army. This last one was kind of a stretch, considering she would wake me up by singing some sweet sounding song every day, as she opened the curtains to let in the early morning sunlight.

We fought imaginary dragons together, until I was too old to believe in such things. And when I was all grown up, we even fought some monsters together that are very real to this very day. Her prayers replaced toy swords, when reality came to call.

I see the same relationship between my wife and her sons today. And this is why I still have to laugh a bit whenever I see the word Reverend in front of my name on a funeral bulletin or wedding program, because these two ladies are the greatest ministers I will ever know. I am also sure that God has placed someone in your life like this as well, so pray within the Holy Spirit and take a healthy look back, because ultimately we all have at least one: *Psalm 59: 16-17 (NIV): But I will sing of your strength, in the morning I will sing of your love; for you are my fortress, my refuge in times of trouble. O my Strength, I sing praise to you; you, O God, are my fortress, my loving God.*

One last word in regard to my mother and this one's from my father; one of his perfect shells: "Just don't do anything that would ever break your mother's heart." This is a pretty tall order, whenever you deal with perfection, and may only be accomplished by the One who created those perfect shells, with the power of the Holy Spirit.

PRAYER POINT:

Train me in hope and strengthen my faith, as I enable the past to remain behind me, and now become: One in the Spirit.

AISLE THIRTEEN
Joy and Peace

Hope gives wings to the imagination and faith lends the power to fly.

Luke 8: 45-48 (NIV): "Who touched me?" Jesus asked. When they all denied it, Peter said, "Master, the people are crowding and pressing against you." But Jesus said, "Someone touched me; I know that power has gone out from me." Then the woman, seeing that she could not go unnoticed, came trembling and fell at his feet. In the presence of all the people, she told why she had touched him and how she had been instantly healed. Then he said to her, "Daughter, your faith has healed you. Go in peace."

*H*ow fitting that the last "Leave on Shelf," back on Aisle Twelve, contained the term: "I may not be able to do this." And, the simple fact of the matter is, "you're right!" You, emphasis on: "You", will never be able to do this, as long as you do not access and utilize the Holy Spirit.

Christ even told his disciples, the night he was betrayed: *Matthew 26:41: (NIV): "Watch and pray with me so you do not fall into temptation. The spirit is willing but the flesh is weak."* I have to admit that sometimes my flesh can be so weak I am amazed that I am not bursting at the seams. Check that last sentence, as it is usually most of the time that I am bursting at my thin skin seams. But it is during these weak moments, I need to remember the One who formed that weak outer shell is also the One who gave me his Spirit: *Isaiah 44: 2-3 (NIV): This is what the Lord says, he who made you, who formed you in the womb, and who will help you: Do not be afraid, O Jacob my servant, Jeshurun, whom I have chosen. For I will pour water on the thirsty land and streams on the dry ground; I will pour out my Spirit on your offspring, and my blessing on your descendants."* Translation: The next time you feel like you may not have the courage to push that second or third drink back, or in my case "the first," take heart, or take the Spirit within your heart, and realize that the One who created you will not let you go thirsty.

Now, as we head toward the check out, let me leave you with one last one for the proverbial road, so to speak. *Romans 14: 17-18 (NIV): "For the kingdom of God is not a matter of eating and drinking, but of righteousness, peace and joy in the Holy Spirit, because anyone who serves Christ in this way is pleasing to God and approved by men."* I believe this one just about says it all. Within these two verses in Paul's letter to the Romans, we have the reminder that we will not find any lasting joy in what we eat or drink. As a matter of fact, no joy will be found in these practices outside of basic human sustenance, as they offer a fleeting and temporary happiness at best. Yes, they may make you happy for a while, but happiness is a fair weather friend when compared to the true and eternal nature of God's joy through the Holy Spirit. We soon discover that we have engaged once again in the proverbial "Three Step"; one step forward and two steps back. Paul doesn't leave us in the "bar and grill" for long though, as he immediately tabs us out and sends us through the front door with righteousness, peace and joy in the Holy Spirit. Then, as if to wave goodbye to an old friend as he pulls away from the neon glow of the parking lot, he assures us that our choice is not only pleasing to God, but will also be condoned by our old buddies, given the fact that they are our true friends indeed: *"pleasing to God and approved by men."*

When you boil it down or shake and stir, whatever your case may be, it really is so simple a "child" could understand it: *Luke 10: 21 (NIV): At that time Jesus, full of joy through the Holy Spirit, said, "I praise you, Father, Lord of heaven and earth, because you have hidden these things from the wise and learned, and revealed them to little children. Yes, Father, for this was your good pleasure."* And therefore, I would assume Paul considered the Galatians to be a bunch of wise guys, because he lays it out for them repeatedly: *Galatians 5: 16-18 (NIV) "So I say, live by the Spirit, and you will not gratify the desires of the sinful nature. For the sinful nature desires what is contrary to the Spirit and the Spirit what is contrary to the sinful nature. They are in conflict with each other, so that you do not do what you want. But if you are led by the Spirit, you are not under the law."*

The fact that we find this comparison of the Holy Spirit's power and attributes to those of the sinful nature so many times in the New Testament, often followed by the dismal final results of the latter, would almost make us conceited as we pursue this abundant lifestyle. Jesus puts it in perspective, in *Luke 10: 17-20 (NIV)*, as he offers the disciples the "eternal caveat" to this new found power: *The seventy-two returned with joy and said, "Lord, even the demons submit to us in your name." He replied, "I saw Satan fall like lightning from heaven. I have given you authority to trample on snakes and scorpions and to overcome all the power of the enemy; nothing will harm you. However, do not rejoice that the spirits submit to you, but rejoice that your names are written in heaven."* Now, before you think I may have handed you the wrong map here, let me explain the marching orders in a little further detail. Christ was telling them what we all need to know, and that is the fact that we are given the Holy Spirit as a "seal of approval" once we have accepted the sacrifice of Jesus Christ on the cross for our sins. The Holy Spirit is a power source and he was given to us from Christ, as a collateral gift of our salvation and righteousness, made possible through the sacrifice of Christ. Paul defines this for us in *2 Timothy 1:14 (NIV): "Guard the good deposit that was entrusted to you –guard it with the help of the Holy Spirit that lives in us."* The *"good deposit"* is abundant life in our earthly body as well as eternal life when our days on this earth are completed. *"Guard the good deposit,"* in this instance, does not mean we are contending for eternal life, because that is guaranteed, once and for all, by our acceptance of Jesus Christ as our personal Savior. The "good deposit" speaks to the degree of your abundant life here on earth, which is very dependent upon you accessing and utilizing the power of the Holy Spirit.

We rest in the assurance that we are not only saved by the mercy and grace of Jesus Christ through our faith in him, but we have the power of the Holy Spirit to negate the fears of this world, and grow in his love. *1 John 4: 13-18 (NIV): "We know that we live in him and he in us, because he has given us of his Spirit. And we have seen and testify that the Father has sent his Son to be the Savior of the world. If anyone acknowledges that Jesus is the Son of God, God lives in him and he in God. And so we know and rely on the love God has for us. God is love. Whoever lives in love, lives in God, and God in him. In this way, love is made complete among us so that we will have confidence on the day of judgment, because in this world we are like him. There is no fear in love, but perfect love drives out fear, because fear has to do with punishment. The one who fears is not made perfect in love."*

The One that paid for this heavenly pass is the same One that hands you the key to abundant life this side of paradise: Jesus Christ and his gift of the Holy Spirit. Our only obligation, if one could even call it that, is to guard the house. The only One that can adequately guard the house is the One that is in the house. Paul explains it like this in *1 Corinthians 6:19 (NIV): Do you not know that your bodies are temples of the Holy Spirit, who is in you, whom you have received from God? You are not your own; you were bought at a price. Therefore, honor God with your bodies.* The only way you can do this long term, with no fear or anxiety attached, is to call upon the Holy Spirit, remembering he is already in the house you are assigned to guard. So there is really no fear factor in any of this. It really is so simple a kid could do it, that is, if you become like a child.

Speaking of being a kid, I remember my father always wore flip-flops around the house. Sometimes, late at night, when I had already been asleep for quite a while, he would come up the stairs to his bedroom, and the "clicking" of those flip-flops in a kind of dream state, would make me realize that I was safe and secure with him there, and there was no fear in the darkness. A few years ago, barely awakened in the middle of the night, I heard the "clicking" of those flip-flops again, and was able to drift right back to sleep, even though my father has been in heaven for over twenty five years. I recalled that moment, that "awakening" the next morning, as well as the peaceful and secure feeling I had which allowed me to go back to sleep. But then realized in the dim light of the early dawn, that the sound I had heard in the middle of that dark night was the "clicking" of the ceiling fan. It really did not matter though, because the security of that moment was provided by the memory of my father, or one could perhaps say, by my Father's Spirit, because we are one within the Spirit. We all have a Father in heaven, and he has given us his Spirit, and the Spirit drives out fear. *Psalm 3:5 (NIV): "I lie down and sleep; I wake again, because the Lord sustains me."* Remember the Holy Spirit is on call twenty-four-seven: *Psalm 16:7 (NIV): I will praise the Lord who counsels me; even at night my heart instructs me.*

As we pursue this new found joy, it would be very advantageous to remember this is "a work in progress." This is a "lifestyle" and not a "crash diet." Paul tells the folks that have observed his trials and tribulations in *Philippians 1: 18-19 (NIV): "Yes, and I will continue to rejoice, for I know that through your prayers and the help given by the Spirit of Jesus Christ, what has happened to me will turn out for my deliverance."* In other words, Paul is acknowledging the fact that there will be skirmishes, battles and wars within this lifetime, but through prayer in the Holy Spirit, the victory will ultimately be ours every time. The additional good news here is that your victories will be witnessed by your family and friends, which will further serve to not only glorify God, but just may be the difference in their collateral blessings and freedom as well. *2 Corinthians 3:3 (NIV): "You show that you are a letter from Christ, the result of our ministry, written not with ink but with the Spirit of the living God, not on tablets of stone, but on tablets of human hearts."* So, as it turns out, "etched in stone" is not as permanent as we once thought, because everything on this earth has a tendency to either fade away or just die. But you have the real deal, as Christ explains in *John 6:63 (NIV): "The Spirit gives life; the flesh counts for nothing. The words I have spoken to you are Spirit and they are life."*

Ask, seek, and knock, and continue to do these three in prayer, receiving the full power and love of the Holy Trinity: God the Father, Jesus Christ the Son, and the Holy Spirit:

Ask for freedom:

2 Corinthians 3:17 (NIV): "Now the Lord is the Spirit, and where the Spirit of the Lord is, there is freedom." This is true freedom, not the kind generations after generations sing songs about before they discover they have to trade it for the most part if they want things like a roof over their head, food to eat and clothing for their children and themselves. This is freedom from within, because it was implanted in you by the One who created you; the same One that knows how your story ends before it ever begins. And he has given you the Holy Spirit, who enables you to face this daunting task we call life with a driving peace from a joy that never ends. This is true freedom. This is what you were born for; to love and be loved by God, and to rest within that love and within that Spirit in all circumstances of life. Welcome to the family of Christ! Or, as Christ states in *John 8: 34-36 (NIV): Jesus replied, "I tell you the truth, everyone who sins is a slave to sin. Now a slave has no permanent place in the family, but a son belongs to it forever. So if the Son sets you free, you will be free indeed.* Yes! Welcome home all of you sons and daughters, welcome back to your true home, and rest in the abundance of joy and the peace of eternal life.

Seek your true identity:

2 Corinthians 3:18 (NIV): "And we, who with unveiled faces all reflect the Lord's glory, are being transformed into his likeness with ever – increasing glory, which comes from the Lord, who is the Spirit. " If you want to truly "discover yourself," this is it. "Finding oneself," that is after you found your freedom, was the second "buzz phrase" of my generation. At the end of the day, at least for my generation, the only thing we discovered in the buzz phrase of finding one's true self, was the dull and mundane buzz of everyday life, as we soon gave up and gave in to the business of making a living. We soon came to the realization that there was not much living to that kind of life at all. Then, after we all woke up from the buzz, or at least those of us that did not disappear into that cloud of smoke never to be seen or heard from again, we soon realized that the "self" we were trying to discover was not really the person we wanted to spend the rest of our lives with, much less carry into mid-life, where goals along with people seem to shift quite a bit. Or in other words, to get back to the *"unveiled faces"* Paul speaks to in *2 Corinthians*, we discovered that through the process of becoming ourselves, we had actually masked our true Spirits. If we are to truly discover ourselves, if we want to define what we are truly intended to be, then that search, that quest and that journey must begin with the realization that we may only achieve this by the transformation into the likeness of Christ. The only possible way that is going to happen is through the power of the

Holy Spirit, as you continue to discover his Word (Holy Bible) and apply it to each and every circumstance of your life.

Knock on the door of joy and peace:

Romans 15:13 (NIV): "May the God of hope fill you with all joy and peace as you trust in him, so that you may overflow with hope by the power of the Holy Spirit." Yes, hope gives wings to the imagination and faith lends the power to fly. When we knock on the door of our own heart, beckoning the power of the Holy Spirit, we soon realize that this is the place we have always imagined. This is our true dream home. This is the place we have always yearned for, even when we were unable to define it within the limited terms of our own human nature.

Go forward in peace, and discover the true joy in the Spirit; being a child of God through faith, hope and love, and remembering that the greatest of these is love. Take up this new life, casting childish things away, which will enable you to live like a child within a kingdom that never grows old. *Psalm 33: 3-6 (NIV): "Sing to him a new song; play skillfully, and shout for joy. For the word of the Lord is right and true; he is faithful in all he does. The Lord loves righteousness and justice; the earth is full of his unfailing love. By the word of the Lord were the heavens made, their starry host by the breath of his mouth."* And remember the Spirit within the realm of your Salvation: *Ephesians 4: 3-6 (NIV): "Make every effort to keep the unity of the Spirit through the bond of peace. There is one body and one Spirit—just as you were called to one hope when you were called—one Lord, one faith, one baptism; one God and Father of all, who is over all and through all and in all."*

LEAVE ON SHELF:

Worries about the present and future, as well as regret over the past are now part of your history.

ADD TO CART:

The joy of abundant life through the Holy Spirit; the life God created you to live, is now yours through faith, and within that faith the power of the Holy Spirit extends the peace of eternal life.

The Holy Spirit is calling you to move forward, with a loving and familiar voice: *Psalm 23: 4-6 (NIV): Even though I walk through the valley of the shadow of death, I will fear no evil, for you are with me; your rod and your staff, they comfort me. You prepare a table before me in the presence of my enemies. You anoint my head with oil; my cup overflows. Surely goodness and love will follow me all the days of my life, and I will dwell in the house of the Lord forever.*

PRAYER POINT:

Give thanksgiving for the Son, who died on the cross for your sins, and rose again, so that you may have eternal and abundant life through the Holy Spirit.

CHECK-OUT

The Holy Spirit

*W*ould you like a sack for that? But there is really no need, because you won't be carrying all of this baggage. And there is no charge today, as you continue to accept and define the priceless gift of the Holy Spirit within your own life. You may take your seat at the ultimate banquet, this is your time; the time of your life.

John 7: 37-39 (NIV): On the last and greatest day of the Feast, Jesus stood and said in a loud voice, "If anyone is thirsty, let him come to me and drink. Whoever believes in me, as the Scripture has said, streams of living water will flow from within him." By this he meant the Spirit, whom those who believed in him were later to receive. Up to that time the Spirit had not been given, since Jesus had not been glorified.

So there you have it, the Spirit is yours for the taking. And thank you for visiting *The Spirit Shop* today, and please come back again.

1 Corinthians 2: 9-12 (NIV): However, as it is written: "No eye has seen, no ear has heard, no mind has conceived what God has prepared for those who love him" – but God has revealed it to us by his Spirit. The Spirit searches all things, even the deep things of God. For who among men knows the thoughts of God except the Spirit of God. We have not received the spirit of the world but the Spirit who is from God, that we may understand what God has freely given us. You have been given the very best of both worlds: Abundant Life and Eternal Life. Now, go forward with courage and confidence through the power of the Holy Spirit within you. This is my prayer for you in the name of Jesus Christ.

Galatians 13:14 (NIV): May the grace of the Lord Jesus Christ, and the love of God, and the fellowship of the Holy Spirit be with you all.

Yours in the Spirit, Amen and Amen.

BIBLIOGRAPHY:

The Holy Bible, New International Version Copyright 1973, 1978, 1984 by International Bible Society:

"Scripture taken from the HOLY BIBLE, NEW INTERNATIONAL VERSION. Copyright 1973, 1978, 1984 International Bible Society. Used by permission of Zondervan Bible Publishers."

Published by The Zondervan Corporation, Grand Rapids, Michigan 49506, U.S.A.

The Holy Bible, Holman Self Pronouncing Red Letter Edition, Copyright 1942 by A.J. Holman Co. Philadelphia, PA. U.S. A.

Made in the USA
Charleston, SC
14 August 2016